STO

ACPL ITEM
DISCARDED

3 1833 00300 1655

Y0-BXV-284

JAN 19 '78

Stephen Harris, in a vivid and incisive account, demonstrates how political economists—even those who are critics of capitalism—have always subscribed to certain basic assumptions that continue to dominate contemporary approaches to problem solving and planning. He shows that explanations of how the economy works, which are based on these assumptions, fail to provide any meaningful solutions to the critical contemporary problems of resource destruction, social costs, human motivation, monopoly, and growth; and argues that these problems will increasingly undermine capital's role of midwife in the quest for expanding wealth and progress.

THE DEATH OF CAPITAL

THE
DEATH
OF CAPITAL

Stephen E. Harris

Pantheon Books, New York

Copyright © 1977 by Stephen E. Harris

All rights reserved under International and Pan-American Copyright Conventions. Published in the United States by Pantheon Books, a division of Random House, Inc., New York, and simultaneously in Canada by Random House of Canada Limited, Toronto.

Library of Congress Cataloging in Publication Data

Harris, Stephen E., 1943–
  The Death of Capital.

  Includes bibliographical references and index.
  1. Capitalism. 2. Economics—History. 3. Economic history—1945– I. Title.
HB501.H358 1977   330.12'2   77-5302
ISBN 0-394-40272-3

Grateful acknowledgment is made to the following for permission to reprint previously published material:

American Association for the Advancement of Science and the author: Specified excerpts from "Photosynthesis and Fish Production in the Sea" by John H. Ryther. Reprinted from *Science*, Vol. 166, pages 72–76, 3 October 1969. Copyright © 1969 by the American Association for the Advancement of Science.

Challenge: Specified excerpt from *Challenge*, March-April 1976 issue, page 67. Published by M. E. Sharpe, Inc., White Plains, N.Y. 10603

Consumers Union: Specified excerpt from the article "Ma Bell's Consumer Reform Bill." Reprinted from *Consumer Reports*, January 1977 issue. Copyright © 1977 by Consumer Union of United States, Inc., Mount Vernon, N.Y. 10550.

Harper & Row, Publishers, Inc.: Specified excerpts from *Capitalism, Socialism and Democracy*, 3rd Edition by Joseph A. Schumpeter. Copyright 1942, 1947 by Joseph A. Schumpeter. Copyright 1950 by Harper & Row, Publishers, Inc.

Alfred A. Knopf, Inc.: Specified excerpts from pages 144–146 and 273 of *The Closing Circle: Nature, Man and Technology* by Barry Commoner. Copyright © 1971 by Barry Commoner. Portions of this book were first published in *The New Yorker*.

The New York Review of Books: Specified excerpt from an essay by S. R. Eyre which was published in the November 18, 1971 issue of *The New York Review of Books.* Copyright © 1971 by NYREV, Inc.

The Texas Quarterly: Specified excerpts from the article entitled "Non-Fuel Mineral Resources in the Next Century" by T. S. Lovering. Reprinted from *The Texas Quarterly*, Summer 1968 issue. Copyright © 1968 by *The Texas Quarterly.*

Manufactured in the United States of America

First Edition

For Nina, Jenny and Terry

1987528

CONTENTS

CHARTS AND TABLES

PREFACE

A new spectre is haunting capital. Puzzling forms of crisis have emerged. Our cherished beliefs in free enterprise and scientific progress are challenged. A short while ago capital promised us an abundant future. Now there may be no future at all.

Economists, for all their technical treatises on inflation, unemployment, monetary crises and trade deficits, are at a loss to explain what is happening. Anticapitalist critiques of imperialism, war, poverty, racism and sexism touch mainly the symptoms. A fresh analysis is needed, whose purpose is not to detail the mechanics of capital, or to reveal its sins. We must reexamine the postulates of the classical theory to find what went wrong, and to gain a new understanding which will help us to lift the nightmare of our future.

But first, what is the "capital" that we speak of? The broadest meaning of the term is that of an accumulated body of ways and means—language, habits, and techniques—passed down from father to son, from mother to daughter, without which no culture, however primitive, could exist. In a more restricted sense, capital refers to those embodiments of past labor known as "tools"—whether flint axes, bows, tractors, or blast furnaces—which are a means to enhance current production.

When we talk of "the death of capital" we do not speak of capital in either of these senses. These forms of capital are synonymous with human existence.

The most obvious distinction of modern capital is quantitative. It is characteristic of "capitalist" industry and commerce that it "requires a larger unit of material equipment than one individual can compass by his own labor, and larger than one person can make use of alone."[1] An immediate corollary is that modern capital is useless without "workers," those who have no independent means, and hence must labor for those who control the capital. To the worker, then, not only is the acquisition of modern material equipment beyond the compass of individual effort; the products of his labor, as capital, are transformed into an alien power which returns to dominate him.

Modern economists like to speak in dry facts and figures, abstracted from their social setting. But it is usually in commonplace issues, not in obscure mathematical formulae, that political economy holds its deepest truths. The division between those who do the work and those who control it, for example, has significance beyond that of determining who gets what share of the booty. It should alert us to the fact that we cannot talk of the phenomenon of capital apart from the industrial and social order—capitalism—in which it arose and to which it gives shape. Capital is more than a profitable investment. It is a dynamic process created out of a unique set of historic circumstances.

Our capital is a curious phenomenon. It can be as substantial as a network of factories and warehouses employing tens of thousands, or it can be as intangible as the name on a soda bottle or an entry in an account. Above all, capital is a force, a quest for wealth and control that has gripped nations, built cities and railroads, conquered old worlds, settled new ones, and opened up an era of discovery and invention. Marx wrote, "Capital is the economic power that dominates everything in bourgeois society."[2] It will go anywhere, do anything, to attain greatness and glory.

Since this gigantic power that embraces all and changes everything is not just a material phenomenon but a social and psychological one as well, it is not easy to grasp. To unveil the source of capital's might, we will journey back to the classical period of political economy of Adam Smith and his successors. They were the first to grapple with capital, and to explore the dynamics of competitive enterprise. Despite the criticisms that have been advanced over the past two centuries refuting or refining their doctrines, the political-economic models created by the founding fathers, for better and for worse, are essentially those in use by economists today.

Karl Marx sought to discover the limits to capital. He was a master of his subject, and brought to it an analytic depth and historic vision that was absent from the increasingly arid reasoning of his contemporaries. What is not usually appreciated is that Marx was very much a part of the classical tradition from which he sought to escape. From our present point of view, his political economy shares many of the limitations of the classical school.

Part II of this book is an in-depth criticism of the classical theory. It examines the underlying postulates of the classical model, most of which, in the final analysis, have been ignored by defenders and detractors of capital alike. One of the main contentions of this book is that until we become acquainted with the presumptions and limitations of the classical model, we will not be able to understand how capital works, or where it fails, today.

The final chapters apply these criticisms to the traditional notions of industrial progress and economic growth. We see how economic evolution leads to structural decay, and we ferret out the real significance of capitalist planning. Most of all, we will find out why capital has a bleak future, in spite of its glorious past.

ACKNOWLEDGMENTS

Thanks to:

Dr. Irene Till, for her constant guidance and criticism.

Dr. Catherine R. Harris, for reading my manuscript, and for our stimulating discussions on Marx, ecology, and other topics.

Susan Gyarmati, for editing the book and prodding the intellect.

My wife, Marsha, for giving many hours of her time to reading and typing the manuscript. Her advice was invaluable in excising irrelevant passages, improving the arguments, and producing a more readable book.

Part 1
SETTING
THE STAGE

1

The State of
the Art

When you have eliminated all which is impossible, then whatever remains, however improbable, must be the truth.

Sherlock Holmes

The problems of political economy have extended far beyond the grasp of the intellectual implements designed to comprehend them. We face inflation and recession, energy shortages, unemployment, urban decay, crime, corruption, diminished resources, and ecological devastation. We fear not just an economic collapse similar to the Depression of the 1930s, but a loss of control over our destiny. Our way of life, our very survival, seems threatened. It would appear that capital is hacking, plowing, paving, spraying, bulldozing, shooting, dumping, and blasting our way to oblivion.

The failure to come up with a meaningful analysis of these problems is in part due to deliberate design and a comfortable acquiescence by the economic profession. The demand for economic brain-workers, after all, is created by the need to apply economic principles to achieve limited institutional objectives. Educational and research organizations are not exempt from these constraints, since they were created to serve more or less the same institutional demands. Professors come and go between teaching, government, and industry. Their students receive professional training to do similar work. Research grants and consulting jobs are not given out for the purpose of discovering alternatives to the existing political-economic order.[1]

Another constraint on the imagination of economists is the nature of their professionalism. They want economics to be a science. And science to them does not admit to cumulative changes in individual or collective behavior. Passion or politics, even ignorance, have no place in their economics. Other disciplines, such as sociology, history, geology, or biology, are not allowed to encroach upon their academic preserve. Instead, economists have a penchant for developing elaborate technique which, as Bernard D. Nossiter put it, is nothing more than "an elegant mathematical facade to cloak the poverty of imagination."[2] To create surrogate human beings counting their "utils" (elementary particles of happiness) or finding their way with "indifference maps" is a pathetic exercise. To call such vacant abstraction a "science" is a delusion.

Any true social science must have a sense of historic purpose and employ tools and techniques suited to the phenomena which the scientists wish to comprehend. In no science are the forces, processes, and relationships more varied and complex than in political economy. Any catalog of the barest minimum of historical, technical, political, social, psychological, and biological detail which political economy must encompass would indicate the need for integrative and inductive reasoning of a high order. As for the economists themselves, they must be renaissance thinkers, not narrow-minded scholastics.

The narrow, defensive method of economics is better suited to ignoring, than controlling, historic events. Capitalism is now beset with too many problems to be portrayed as a natural, universal order, even in the abstract. Yet conservative and liberal economists treat these problems as though they are either exogenous to the system, or difficulties of a minor order to which the system can adjust. The choice of the term "externalities," to refer to the inability of the market to optimize social costs and prudently manage our resources, indicates that such malfunctions are of secondary importance and need not upset their analytic harmony unduly. Publishers of economic texts append chapters on poverty, urban problems, race, the environment, "comparative" economics, the Third World, and "radical" economics as if they were baubles on a Christmas tree.

What never occurs to the average economist is that the free exercise of the power of capital, not its curtailment, is the root cause of capitalist decay. The acceptance of this proposition would force economists to cast off from their philosophic moorings—sending them rudderless upon uncharted, stormy waters.

2

The Classical
Theory of Capitalism

Every individual generally, indeed, neither intends to promote
the public interest, nor knows how much he is promoting it. By
preferring the support of domestic to foreign industry, he intends
only his own security; and by directing that industry in such a
manner as its produce may be of the greatest value, he intends
only his own gain, and he is in this, as in many other cases, led
by an invisible hand to promote an end which was no part of his
intention.

Adam Smith

Until we know how capitalism works, it will be difficult to understand how diminishing resources or growing social ills impinge upon
the system. Will capitalism adapt to the needs of the next century?
Will it be transformed? Destroyed?

To find the answers, we had best begin with the classical theory
of political economy. The classical theory is such a brilliant synthesis
of the economics, politics, and morals of capitalism that it has come
to be regarded as the objective perfection against which the everyday
world is measured.

Later on we will see that the classical theory is only a first approximation of today's reality. To understand the future, we will have to
break away from the concepts of the past. But we must start with
an understanding of classical political economy, its origins and assumptions, before we can transcend it. Perhaps that is the test of a
great theory: that it is essential to our understanding even when it
is, strictly speaking, "wrong."

The political economy of capitalism is the political economy of
competitive individualism. Adam Smith's *Wealth of Nations,* written

in 1776, draws us a picture of individuals struggling through hard work and shrewd bargaining to better their lot. The neoclassical economists of the late 1800s brought that image into sharp focus with their mathematical theories of competitive equilibrium which showed individuals reacting to conditions over which they had no control. When the realities of economic power demanded a more sophisticated view, economists adapted to the world of "imperfect" and "monopolistic" competition.

Whatever its modifications, the notion of competition has always served as the key concept in economic theory. All other theories and concepts—including those of value, price, supply and demand, income distribution, investment, and interest—are either directly or indirectly derived from the theory of competition. Competition adjusts employment and output to their proper level, spurs economic growth, and fosters invention.

To what do we owe the importance of the competitive concept? To answer this question, we must review the evolution of economic science in the context of the history of capitalism.

Modern political economy took form in the eighteenth century, when commercial capitalists and manufacturers were struggling for power in England and Western Europe. The economists championed the bourgeois cause in demanding an end to feudal privileges and elimination of the monopolies of the guilds and merchants. They fought for a world of free trade and ever-expanding markets. The philosophers of capitalism were the champions of progress.

That "progress" had not always come easily. The birth of capitalism was, as Karl Marx put it, "anything but idyllic." The primary accumulation of "capital" to get capitalism rolling was not, for the most part, the product of frugality. It was the loot from Spanish mines in Mexico and Peru that filled the coffers of the merchants and bankers of Europe—money that was used to underwrite empires, equip trading expeditions, open mines, and manufacture armaments. When Britain became the leading power and laid hands on its share of the booty, it did so through such genteel means as the slave trade, opium wars, the conquest of India, and other civilizing ventures. Commerce was the mother of invention and industry; war and pillage, the midwife.

Before the competitive system could work, there also had to be workers. Hard-pressed as the peasants were by rents and taxes, they were not ready to flock to the mines and factories. In fifteenth-century England there were no more serfs; in their place stood free peasant proprietors who worked their few acres of land and grazed their cattle on the commons. The towns, too, had grown into independent, prosperous centers of trade and guild production. Their monopolistic practices and rigid rules were not hospitable to free enterprising capitalist manufacturers.

Before the influx of merchant wealth could be turned into modern capital, it had an important role to play in undermining the old society. In the sixteenth and seventeenth centuries the flood of gold and silver from the Americas caused a price revolution throughout Europe which wreaked havoc with the slower-moving agrarian and handicraft economy of the time, sending thousands begging. At the end of the fifteenth century a French worker's wages had bought 4.3 kilograms of meat; a century later, the same wages would buy only 1.8 kilograms. In the England of 1495, a peasant could earn enough wages in fifteen weeks to provision his household for a year. By 1610 he could work the entire year and still not earn enough to buy the same amount of goods.[1]

As a result of the price revolution, the practice of "rack-renting" had to be introduced to protect the income of the landowners:

> Rents of land and the fines paid when a new tenant took over a holding had been practically stationary. They had been fixed by custom—and in the past custom had had the force of law. But now that the revolution in prices necessitated a greater return from his land . . . the lord jacked up the rent so high that the tenant often found it impossible to pay and had to give up his land.[2]

If inflated rents were not enough to drive the peasants from the land, all pretense of respect for their feudal rights was cast aside and they were evicted from the soil by force. The enclosure movement in England was pushed forward by the same commercial forces that were bringing the rapid expansion of trade and colonial plunder:

> In insolent conflict with king and parliament, the great feudal lords created an incomparably larger proletariat by the forcible driving of the peasantry from the land, to which the latter had the same feudal right as the lord himself, and by the usurpation of the common lands. The rapid rise of the Flemish wool manufactures, and the corresponding rise in the price of wool in England, gave the direct impulse to these evictions.[3]

This process of expropriation and theft was carried on from the last third of the fifteenth century to the end of the eighteenth. This

period took in the Protestant Reformation, during which church
lands were also confiscated, and along with the land the rights of
their tenants. It also witnessed the large-scale theft and sale of state
property.[4]

By expelling peasants from the soil, the agricultural revolution
helped to lay the foundation for the Industrial Revolution. The
once-proud yeomen of England who were "freed" from an independent livelihood were then forced onto the market by strict laws
against paupers and vagabonds. From the beginning, poverty and
industry were intimately linked.

As industry took hold, much of its human raw material was inter-
nally generated, again through pauperization. The new system of
work reduced the craftsman to a wage-earner. The products of the
factory system ran handicrafts out of the market, destroying the
organization and security of the guilds. Men, women, and children
had no choice but to serve in the woolen mills of Leeds or the iron
works of Shropshire. Thus, in the name of property, great masses of
people were deprived of their rights to till the soil or saw the ruin
of their trade.

Dark beginnings for the Age of Enlightenment.

But in this crucible of turmoil and conflict, a new society was being
forged. The classical political economists believed that the manufacturing system would usher in an era of individual freedom and
unprecedented prosperity. Liberty and freedom of contract for the
individual; unfettered trade and free competition for the employer.
This paradox of harmonious conflict was the key to progress and
prosperity. Adam Smith maintained:

> The natural effort of every individual to better his own condition,
> when suffered to exert itself with freedom and security, is so powerful
> a principle, that it is alone, and without any assistance, . . . capable
> of carrying on the society to wealth and prosperity.[5]

It was a bold—one might even say daring—concept. The philosophers of capitalism not only accepted the selfish, avaricious nature
of human beings; they asserted that any actions inhibiting men's base
instincts, well-meaning as they were, would only lead to the detri-
ment of the common weal.

Why? Because such actions unbalance the economic mechanism.
The laws of competition, if allowed to operate freely, keep the harmful propensities of individuals in check. If a worker is paid less than

his labor is worth by a miserly employer, he is free to go to another employer who will pay more and profit by it. Should a supplier attempt to charge an excessive price, others will step in to provide the product cheaper.

Thus the unfettered interplay of avaricious instincts leads to a stalemate of forces and an allocation of society's resources according to the demands of the marketplace.

Once productive relationships have been established, can they then be fixed by fiat so as to avoid further conflict? The classical economists would answer no. They recognized that "free and universal competition" was a dynamic process—an ever-changing interplay of forces which was relentlessly propelling itself toward greater productivity, new and richer markets. In a continuous battle against uncertainty, the weak would be weeded out from the strong. "For the sake of self-defence,"[6] each contributor to the economic process could be compelled to strive to his utmost ability. This way, capitalist production became a dynamic process which promoted continual advances in productive techniques and a never-ending augmentation of wealth.

In the eyes of Adam Smith and his followers, the statesman could be no substitute for the entrepreneur, despite the fact that though the investor of capital seeks only his private profit, considerations of society's gain "never enter into his thoughts."[7] The market served as a gigantic laboratory in which countless individuals weighed their risks and opportunities, selected the course in their best interests, then reevaluated their actions in light of the results. Through this process of continuous interaction and adjustment, society's resources could be allocated with a wisdom that no individual or body politic could possess.[8]

Liberty, then, was to be the cornerstone of capitalism; competition, the driving force. Competition served the dual purposes of propelling the manufacturing and industrial system forward and of protecting the rights of individuals. The weak, though deprived of property, would never be reduced to slavery. The strong would be compelled to plow back most of their spoils into productive investments in order to preserve their ability to expropriate. Out of base beginnings came a noble end with material benefits for all. Without competition, the entire system of liberty, harmony and progress was inconceivable. "Only through the principle the competition," wrote John Stuart Mill, "has political economy any pretension to the character of a science."[9] He might have added that without competition, capitalism can have no pretension to the character of a self-regulating system.

Competition was the key to unlocking the forces of capitalist expansion. "Laissez faire" became the battle cry. Armed with their new philosophy, the classical political economists had a program to harness individual avarice to the cart of the common weal and to achieve social harmony through unfettered conflict. They fought against Corn Laws which put an "unnaturally" high price on agricultural products, against bullion regulations which hampered free trade, and against all manner of government interference with industry. With the hindsight of two centuries of capitalist development, it seems that the forces of competition were more powerful than Adam Smith and his followers had imagined.

They were also less harmonious. The squalor of the factory system and the plunder of colonialism were the price one paid for progress. Adam Smith saw the need for public education to overcome the stupefying effects of factory labor. During the nineteenth century, the most ardent protagonists of free trade allowed for public expenditure on sanitation and legislation against child labor, adulterated bread, and fourteen-hour workdays. But with some—not too many—legislated improvements, the system had more than the minimum amount of balanced justice needed to survive the class conflicts it created. Even trade unions, once feared as the organizing agent of class warfare, were seen to have a legitimate role in countering the power of organized capital and in promoting social and industrial order.

Yet there was a hitch. Even if the harmony between capital and labor could be maintained, the industrial system was subject to very real crises which periodically severed the ties of finance and trade, and threatened to undermine the social relations of production. Defenders of capital tried to ignore these crises or attribute them to external, temporary causes such as wars, crop failures, overspeculation or panic. Marx believed that with every triumph of industry and trade, the system would become more vulnerable. He concluded that capitalism was a limited phase of history—an increasingly crisis-prone system that would ultimately collapse.

During the 1930s, even conservative economists were forced to admit that there might be a basic flaw in the classical system. During this period of massive unemployment and the collapse of business confidence, increasing attention was turned to the actual structure of monopolistic institutions, in contrast to the perfect world of the textbooks. Some social scientists were beginning to think that monopoly might be the Achilles heel of capitalism. A. A. Berle and Gardiner Means pointed out that a"corporate revolution" was taking place. That there had been an almost unnoticed "transition of . . . industrial wealth . . . from individual ownership to ownership by the large, publicly financed corporations [which had vitally changed] the lives of property owners, the lives of workers, and the methods of property tenure."[10] The great concern was that the self-regulating market mechanisms which ensured a stable economy, steady growth, and full employment had been shattered by the power of the giant corporations.

How did the corporate revolution affect the classical harmony? In the pure classical system, crises do not exist. Writing in 1814, the French economist J. B. Say had put into "law" the classical belief that production (supply) creates its own demand in a market economy. Say has been unfairly singled out for his naïveté in bluntly saying that "it is production which creates markets for goods."

In effect, this means that the capitalist economy is normally in a state of full employment. There will always be enough jobs: it is just a question of determining the wages that will balance the supply and demand for labor. There will always be enough demand for goods and services: these will be paid for by the same wages and profits that were obtained in their production. Again, it is just a question of finding "through the higgling of the market" the price that equates market supply with demand. Barring wars, panics, or government meddling, the circle of full employment was the normal state of the competitive economy.

But the modern monopolist is not bound by the code of behavior assumed in the classical theory. Faced with a drop in demand, he may opt to cut production rather than lower prices (since there are no competitors to undercut him). Workers could be laid off; total demand in the economy would fall, forcing other industries to make similar cuts. The circle of full employment would be broken and twisted into a downward spiral.

To give a recent example of such behavior, when the demand for aluminum slumped sharply in 1974, the industry held its prices firm and let the output drop. Had the industry been made up of many firms, each acting on its own, price slashes would have been inevitable. During the Depression, Gardiner Means had discovered that prices in agriculture and other competitive industries tumbled, while prices in the automotive, steel, and other concentrated industries held remarkably firm, even in the face of drastic cuts in output and employment.[11]

The obvious solution to this problem was antitrust—break up the monopolies, restore competition, and get the self-regulating market mechanisms working again.

But would the obvious solution work? Two famous studies on the problem of monopoly were published in the early 1930s: one by Joan Robinson, the other by E. H. Chamberlin.[12] Both wished to update economic theory by studying how producers behaved under real-world conditions of "monopolistic" or "imperfect" competition. As Joan Robinson put it, the analysis of monopoly "presented a hard, indigestible lump which the competitive analysis could never swallow."

Surprisingly, both studies reached remarkably ambivalent conclusions. It was found, for example, that it was one thing to study the effect of monopoly on a single isolated industry, but quite another to determine its effect on all industries taken together. In the latter case, the effects that monopolies had on one another tended to cancel out. Production as a whole was not nearly so restricted as it would have appeared to be from adding up the individual cases.

Technology was another factor. In industries where large corporations produce more efficiently than their small competitors, monopolies may turn out more goods at lower prices. (Subsequent studies have shown that large size usually is not conducive to technological innovation.[13]) If monopolies had a more secure market and garnered bigger profits, they thereby had, it was reasoned, greater incentive, and funds to invest. All in all, Robinson and Chamberlin found that monopoly had its dislocating effects, but it alone could not account for the Depression.

It followed, then, that while a vigorous policy of antitrust might help to restore the competitive health of the economy, it was no quick and lasting solution to the problem of unemployment and crisis. In effect, the Robinson-Chamberlin analysis had shown where the trust-busters were in error. They had not taken into account the most basic monopoly of all: the private ownership of capital. If the capitalist class as a whole feared for its profits, investments would fall, no matter how competitive the economy appeared on the surface.

As it turned out, the collapse of capitalism in the West was less imminent than had been feared, or hoped, during the depths of the Depression. Into the breach came the New Deal, World War II arms expenditures, and one of the great intellectual rescue operations of all time: Keynes's *General Theory of Employment, Interest, and Money.*

Rather than replace the outdated classical model of competitive capitalism by building a new theory from the ground up (as Means, Robinson, and Chamberlin were attempting to do), Keynes stepped outside the classical theory to come up with a political solution to the problem of unemployment. With hardly a mention of monopoly, Keynes reasoned that the normal state of affairs is one in which there is a gap between aggregate supply and aggregate demand. He took it for granted that Say's Law of Markets was no longer valid. That being the case, Keynes reasoned it was up to government to supply the proper mix of fiscal and monetary policies to bridge the gap and keep employment at a high level. If capital was afraid to take risks, government would underwrite the economy with deficit spending. If high interest rates discouraged investors, the money supply would be increased. The tax rate could be moved up and down. Government jobs could be created. Economists were given a whole bag of tools to work with in "fine-tuning" the economy.[14]

After performing this magnificent act of academic legerdemain to solve the problem of unemployment, Keynes quickly stepped back into the best-of-all-possible-worlds of competitive capitalism:

> If our central controls succeed in establishing an aggregate volume of output corresponding to full employment as nearly as practicable, the classical theory comes into its own again from this point onwards.[15]

By apparently showing how prosperity could be engineered by government policies, Keynes greatly enhanced the importance and prestige of the economics profession. The postwar era of relatively high employment and rising GNP allowed economists to adopt a comfortably conservative attitude reminiscent of the heyday of laissez faire. Once the government had done its job, Paul Samuelson, for one, could only marvel at how much of economic life goes on without direct government intervention:

> This functioning alone is convincing proof that a competitive system of markets and prices . . . is not a system of chaos and anarchy. There is in it a certain order and orderliness. It works. A competitive system is an elaborate mechanism for unconscious coordination through a system of prices and markets, a communication device for pooling the knowledge and actions of millions of diverse individuals.[16]

The truth of these modified laissez faire doctrines was too obvious to have to justify. Instead of taking the class society and the theory of distribution as the starting point (as the early classical economists had),[17] economic science came to be based upon "partial equilibrium" analysis. In theory, one was supposed to take a single supply-and-demand situation, such as the market for bales of cotton, and extend the analysis to every commodity until a "general equilibrium" for the entire market system was reached. Consumer choice was turned into an elaborate theory of "indifference analysis," the "elasticity" of demand, "substitution effects," and "general consumer's equilibrium." Then it was on to the firm, with the analysis of supply, the equation of "marginal cost" with "marginal revenue," and an achievement of industry-wide competitive equilibrium. The theories of wages, interest, and rent were similarly treated from the standpoint of partial equilibrium analysis, each with their particular terminology but all saying essentially the same thing—the market for every resource or product is equated through the interaction of supply and demand. Put all the "partial equilibria" together and you had general equilibrium as expressed in the theories of employment and growth. The very term "equilibrium" sounds as solid as the British Empire—or the American one to follow.

Keynes, then, is still the economist of monopoly capitalism par excellence. Assured that they could "engineer" prosperity, economists were content during the 1950s and 1960s to tinker with refinements to the neoclassical analysis. True, if the problem of maintaining sufficient demand to assure full employment were the sole—or even the central—problem of monopoly capitalism, perhaps the Keynesian modification of classical political economy would be the last word for the foreseeable future.

It is not. As we will see later, insufficient demand is only one of several problems besetting capitalism, each of which tends to diminish the relevance of classical economic theory. The stunning success of the Keynesian rescue operation may turn out to be, in historical perspective, nothing more than a short-lived holding operation preceding the complete collapse of the eternal laws of classical political economy.

3

The Marxian Scenarios

The laborer ... constantly produces material, objective wealth, but in the form of capital, of an alien power that dominates and exploits him.

Karl Marx

Just as the classical system provided the philosophic basis for the overthrow of the feudal and mercantilist order, so was it suited to capitalism's foremost antagonist, Karl Marx. It was he who brought the logic of competitive capitalism to a full circle. For classical economists, competition would unleash the forces of expansion. For Marx, competition was also the key to the evolution of social relations themselves. In his view, the divisions that grew out of the class structure of competitive capitalism were to become sharper and the conflicts more violent as capital accumulation progressed. Eventually capitalism would be overthrown by the workers, to be replaced with a higher form of social unity.

The relation of Marx's views to those of other classical thinkers tends to be obscured by his advocacy of socialism. The supporters of capitalism generally saw the competition in production as the means to increasing the well-being of all classes of society. Many Socialists, on the other hand, rejected competition altogether as an oppressive system of production and an exploitive manner of distribution. To them the capitalist system should be replaced on moral grounds, either through one of the schemes for social improvement being advanced by various self-appointed leaders of the workers, or through a take-over of industry by the state, acting in the interests of the majority.

Marx rejected this debate between protagonists of capitalism and socialism as artificial and ahistorical. He dissociated himself from those who advocated socialism mainly on moral grounds by branding his way of thinking "scientific" as opposed to "utopian." His purpose was not to win debating points for the Socialists, but to understand the historic role of capitalist production in the evolution of social relations and prepare for the day when the socialist revolution would be successful. Socialism (at least in Western Europe) could only come about through the victory of the working class in the struggle against the bourgeoisie—through seizure of state power and expropriation of capital.

Marx did not believe that history was a purely material process, independent of people's wills. But he did believe that the material forces had to be understood before conscious struggle was possible. It was the task of Socialists both to understand historic forces and to direct them in the interests of the working class.[1]

MARX AND THE CLASSICAL ECONOMISTS

Although Marx was a Socialist whose evolutionary ideas gave him a historical vision that the classical economists lacked, he nevertheless shared many of their ideas. Let's look more closely at some of them.

First, Marx portrayed capitalism as a class society. Was this a novel view? It is hard to find anything more basic to classical theory than the division of society into landowning, capitalist, and laboring classes. Each class had a unique set of economic and political interests, and much of the classical analysis revolved around how the interests of each class competed and conflicted with one another. "As to myself," wrote Marx, "no credit is due to me for discovering either the existence of classes in modern society or the struggle between them. Long before me bourgeois historians had described the historical development of this class struggle and bourgeois economists the economic anatomy of the classes."[2] David Ricardo, in fact, believed that the determination of the laws by which society's produce is divided between the classes—as rent, profit, and wages—was the principal problem of political economy. Marx refined that class analysis of capitalism down to its basic antagonism between workers and owners. For him, the true meaning and significance of the concrete categories of industrial profit, commercial profit, interest, and rent could be grasped only by tracing them back to their common origin in the "surplus value" extracted through the labor process. This basic surplus was the difference between what workers were paid for their labor power and the amount they actually produced for their employers.

During Marx's lifetime, the bourgeois economists were moving in an opposite direction from that which he had taken. While Marx was expanding upon the notion of class conflict, they were busy purging the classical analysis of any note of disharmony. Bourgeois economists minimized the conflicts and contradictions of capitalism with a theory that income is distributed in accordance with each "person's" contribution to the joint productive effort. These "vulgar economists"—as Marx called them—abolished the classical distinction between the production of value and its distribution as revenue. Instead of taking the real relations of capitalist production as their starting point, they conceived the most superficial appearances and illusions to be their real basis. Land, labor, capital, and credit were reduced to colorless "factors" of production. Class divisions were treated as no more than the form of functional specialization that arises out of the modern organization of industry. Competition was simply the market mechanism for assuring the proper balancing of factors and outputs, not "the mobile and restless monopoly"[3] which is constantly overturning the old basis of production. This mechanical view, which was devoid of any social dynamic, may in fact be less orthodox from the classical point of view than the heretical Marxian dialectic.

By the same token, Marx agreed with Adam Smith, who maintained (not consistently) that profits—the return on wages and means of production advanced—are extracted from the produce of labor. They are the rewards of ownership and control. They are not (as modern economists frequently claim) a return for services provided by capital.

Another, and from the present-day point of view, very important, similarity between Marx's views and those of the classical school is that they were both dealing with competitive, not monopoly, capitalism. It is true, as we shall see, that Marx goes far beyond Smith and Ricardo in discovering the laws of modern industry. He shows how the further accumulation of capital leads to greater concentration and centralization. Yet these processes still take place within a competitive business framework.

Marx's view of competition is perhaps best summed up by this passage from *Capital*:

> Free competition brings out the inherent laws of capitalist production, in the shape of external coercive laws having power over every individual capitalist.[4]

Marx certainly did not ignore the monopolies of his day, nor did he believe that competition was at all "perfect." Industrial concentration played an important role in the political polarization of capitalist society. But it is clear that Marx looked for the breakdown of capitalism to occur through economic growth rather than through the extinction of competition, for capitalism to have had its final crisis before capitalist rivalry would have disappeared.

Last, Marx shared the classical belief that the wealth of society grows through the advance of technology and the spread of industry. In fact, he believed that it was the historic mission of capital to revolutionize the forces of production and lay the foundation for the future society of abundance. Marx fervently attacked Malthus for believing that the laws of population and rent condemned the majority of people to poverty. Nor did he agree with Ricardo's contention that the natural limit to agricultural output would eventually check industrial accumulation.[5]

"The *real barrier* of capitalist production," wrote Marx, "is *capital itself.*"[6] The problem with capitalism was not too many people or too little land. It was that bourgeois productive relations were a rigid constraint around a growing industrial and social potential.

To the classical economists, economic laws were the eternal, universal laws of capitalist society. All previous history, for them, was the process of perfecting the capitalist mode. Marx, on the other hand, regarded capitalism as one stage in the unfolding development of social production. Primitive communism, slavery, feudalism, mercantilism, capitalism, socialism, and communism were all distinct stages in the evolution of the mode of production. Each stage had its own laws or principles. Each stage (except communism) had been or would be transcended when the social forces of production developed to the point where they could no longer be contained by the social relations existing at that time. Marx wrote in the preface to *Capital* of his personal mission to "lay bare the economic law of motion of modern society"[7] that would eventually lead to the triumph of socialism.

Marx's *Capital,* then, is distinguished from the works of the classical economists who saw competitive equilibrium as the counterweight to hedonist conflict. In his determination to see the competitive process through to its ultimate conclusion, Marx embraced the inherent conflicts and tensions of capitalist production and saw in them the secret to the emergence of a more civilized order.

CAPITALIST BREAKDOWN AND TRANSFORMATION

Marx disclosed essentially two scenarios by which the breakdown and transformation of capitalism would occur. Both arose out of the same historic process, and they naturally reinforced one another. The first, more striking scenario arose directly out of technological processes: the harnessing of science to industry, and the accumulation and concentration of capital. It began with the "primitive" capital accumulation and expropriation which separated peasants and artisans from control of the means of production and created the conditions for capitalist exploitation. After capitalism became the dominant mode of production, the inexorable laws of competition would lead to the concentration of capital in fewer and fewer hands, and would also create a swelling body of oppressed, degraded, exploited workers whose interests stood in direct opposition to the capitalist order. Meanwhile, the socialization of the productive process through the development of science and technology would increase the complexity and vulnerability of the capitalist machine. In the end, the workers would revolt and take the machinery into their own hands.

We will call this the "social-political scenario."

The second scenario for crisis arose out of the conflict between the drive to accumulate capital (through the exploitation of labor) and the need to constantly expand the market for the products of industry. The gap between accumulation and demand is a continual invitation to crisis. There is a similarity here between Marx's views and modern Keynesian theory, but it is essential to point out that Marx saw this conflict as an irreconcilable contradiction of capitalism, an inevitable result of the exploitation of labor. Counteracting tendencies that put off the crisis would only make it worse in the end.

We will call this the "economic scenario."

Could either of these two scenarios alone—the social-political crisis or the economic crisis—bring about the Socialist transformation? Certainly not the economic crisis alone, since Marx believed that socialism would not come about automatically. Capital had to be deliberately overthrown by the oppressed majority—the working class. And the working class could acquire the consciousness and the will to carry out its historic mission against the wage system only through proper leadership, education, and organization—through the process of class struggle itself.

Yet there can be no question that economic crisis plays an essential part in the struggle for socialism by undermining the power of capital, by widening the gap between the potential and actual achievements of society, and by strengthening the resolve of the laborers.

The two forms of crisis are thus mutually intertwined. Stated philosophically, "At a certain stage of development, the material productive forces of society come into conflict with the existing relations of production. . . ."[8] This is a deceptively simple statement of the complex manner in which the historical process unfolds.

So it is essential to understand both scenarios in order to get a full picture of the process of revolutionary transformation. For our own convenience, we can first look at each form of crisis separately, and recombine them later when we come to evaluate the Marxian scheme as a whole.

THE SOCIAL-POLITICAL SCENARIO

Anyone who imagines that political economy is dull should read the chapter in *Capital* on the "Historical Tendency of Capitalist Accumulation." After describing how the forces of capitalism annihilate all previous forms of property and production, how these forces usurp, "with merciless vandalism, and under the stimulus of passions the most infamous, the most sordid, the pettiest, the most meanly odious" the property of the independent peasant and craftsman, Marx goes on to show how these same all-powerful, inexorable forces that brought capital into being then turn upon and destroy capital. It is a long paragraph, but well work quoting in full:

> As soon as this process of transformation has sufficiently decomposed the old society from top to bottom, as soon as the laborers are turned into proletarians, their means of labor into capital, as soon as the capitalist mode of production stands on its own feet, then the further socialization of labor and further transformation of the land and other

means of production into socially exploited and, therefore, common means of production, as well as the further expropriation of private proprietors, takes a new form. That which is now to be expropriated is no longer the laborer working for himself, but the capitalist exploiting many laborers. This expropriation is accomplished by the action of the immanent laws of capitalist production itself, by the centralization of capital. One capitalist always kills many. Hand in hand with this centralization, or this expropriation of many capitalists by a few, develop, on an ever-extending scale, the cooperative form of the labor-process, the conscious technical application of science, the methodical cultivation of the soil, the transformation of the instruments of labor into instruments of labor only usable in common, the economizing of all means of production by their use as the means of production of combined, socialized labor, the entanglement of all peoples in the net of the world-market, and with this, the international character of the capitalist régime. Along with the constantly diminishing number of the magnates of capital, who usurp and monopolize all advantages of this process of transformation, grows the mass of misery, oppression, slavery, degradation, exploitation; but with this too grows the revolt of the working-class, a class always increasing in numbers, and disciplined, united, organized by the very mechanism of the process of capitalist production itself. The monopoly of capital becomes a fetter upon the mode of production, which has sprung up and flourished along with, and under it. Centralization of the means of production and socialization of labor at last reach a point where they become incompatible with their capitalist integument. Thus integument is burst asunder. The knell of capitalist private property sounds. The expropriators are expropriated.[9]

That in a nut-integument is Marx's social-political scenario of capitalist crisis. First workers are divorced from the means of production—society is divided into the owners of capital on the one hand, and wage-laborers on the other. The competition among rival capitalists then unleashes powerful forces of production in both industry and agriculture. As production grows, and a credit system develops which allows the formation of stock companies, capital becomes ever more concentrated. Labor is welded into a tighter and tighter mass. Oppressed miserably by the powerful magnates of capital, the united mass of laborers realizes its historic mission, sees its opportunity, and seizes power from the capitalists.

Although this is a marvelous abstraction of the genesis and laws of capitalism, the whole scenario raises many questions. In the first place, bad as the laborer's lot is, why should it be growing worse during the very time that we are witnessing an unprecedented growth in the powers of production? To be sure, capital is becoming more concentrated, but that is not sufficient reason to suspend the laws of supply and demand for labor.[10] Even if workers receive a declining share of the total social product, goods are becoming cheaper, and there seems to be no apparent reason why the laborer's standard of living should not remain the same or even improve.

This point is further supported by the fact that that same force which is supposed to overthrow the capitalist régime, the organized proletariat, is a powerful force for improving the lot of the laborer *within* the capitalist system. Marx, in fact, in his address to the General Council of the First International, exhorted his listeners not to allow the struggle for higher wages to distract them from the real battle of abolishing the wage-system itself.[11]

Here we have an important issue. Although Marx's doctrine of class struggle is related to the classical hedonistic calculus (class consciousness plays a comparable role in Marx's system to that which self-interest plays in the classical doctrine), it is a phenomenon of a higher order. For the working class to be an effective revolutionary force, historic class interest must be put before immediate individual or group interest. But why should the perceived interests of each individual worker be identical with the interests of the working class as a whole? How do we make the jump, in other words, from individual hedonism to class consciousness?[12]

For in reality, the working class may be divided into different craft, industrial, and wage groups. They may be sharply segmented according to education, sex, race, and age. They may be prey to nationalism and chauvinism. Most important of all, workers may perceive and act upon their interests to secure better wages and working conditions rather than engage in the struggle to overthrow the régime of capital. Granted the oppression of labor by capital is universal, there is no immediate reason to believe that workers will adopt a universal outlook, any more than the general interest of capitalists should put an end to commercial competition.

The step up from individual to class interests is of great analytic importance. The pitfall lies in the attempt to equate the self-interest (both real and perceived) of the workers with the self-interest (the objective, long-term self-interest) of the working class as a whole. If the two cannot be equated, the route of class struggle can lead us straight back to the classical position of individualism.

Indeed, Marx shows how difficult it is for individuals to even perceive the true relations of capitalist society, let alone to take an attitude of enlightened self-interest and be motivated to participate in a conscious class struggle. Marx's discussion of the subject is usually put under the heading of "alienation."

The more labor is divided up, the more complex it is, the greater is the degree of interdependence and cooperation among the laborers. But their vision, like the labor process itself, becomes fragmented and they can no longer see the labor process as a whole or their role in it. Hence, even though they are working in closer cooperation than ever before, they feel that they are working alone without contributing to a common enterprise or purpose. This feeling of alienation is reinforced under the capitalist mode of production, in which the goal itself—profit—is abstract and external to the worker's desire or experience. The worker, who no longer owns the tools he works with, is subordinated to this goal by the capitalist's command over his livelihood. The pursuit of consumer's satisfactions—whether real or sublimated fantasies—can motivate the worker but cannot restore his loss of social purpose. Hence arises the need for all sorts of pseudo purposes such as jingoism, racism, and the appeal to partisan politics in order to mollify the worker's sense of social deprivation and keep him in his proper place.

The exchange process of bourgeois economy reinforces this sense of alienation. Under simple commodity production, even without full capitalism, each laborer works for himself, not for society. He is not in any social contact with his fellow producers. He asserts himself as a part of society only through the act of exchange. This exchange is the exchange of commodities; only indirectly does it establish a relation among the producers. "Therefore, the relations connecting the labor of one individual with that of the rest appear, not as direct social relations between individuals at work, but as what they really are, material relations between persons and social relations between things."[13]

When the value of commodities is expressed in the form of its universal money equivalent, mystery is added to mystery. Even the perception of a relation between commodities is lost. Instead of being exchanged in their bodily form, commodities are first abstracted into the form of money before being translated back into the equivalent value of commodities received in exchange. Now, not only has the substance of social labor been lost in the commodity, the substance of the commodity itself is melted down into its pure value expression and no longer bears the mark of the carpenter, weaver, smith, or tanner who produced it.

As if that were not reason enough for the workers under capitalism to lose track of their true relations with one another (and the fact that they are exploited), a still newer mystery is added by the peculiar nature of the commodity labor-power, which the worker sells to the capitalist. To the worker, it appears that the wages he receives are equivalent to the full value of his labor-time, while in reality, he has been working gratis for part of the day. To the serf of the Middle Ages who had to work two or three days a week on the lord's demesne, the nature of his exploitation was as visible as it was palpable. The wage earner under capitalism has no obvious way of telling that he is paid for less than the full value of his labor. "All the slave's labor appears as unpaid labor. In wage-labor, on the contrary, even surplus-labor, or unpaid labor, appears as paid."[14]

By the same token, it appears that the products of labor, including any tools or machinery used in producing them, naturally belong to the capitalist. They came into the capitalist's hands through a free exchange or contract between employer and employee. Wages and working conditions, inasmuch as they are regulated by the market, take on an external objective quality independent of the will of either worker or capitalist. The exploitation of the worker is obscured in a mist of free bargaining and natural rights.[15]

Yet despite the fact that individual producers are alienated from one another through the process of exchange, despite its appearance that the wage is equivalent to the full value of labor, despite the many divisions within the working class itself, and despite the fact that the growing social productivity of labor would seem to be opening the way for improvements in the workers' standard of living within the capitalist system—despite those and other impediments, the workers are supposed to abandon their individualism and develop the far-sighted class consciousness to throw themselves not just into the immediate struggle to improve their own lot and that of their fellow workers, but into the long-term battle to overthrow the capitalist system itself.

And that is easier said than done. Revolution, when it comes, is not for the faint-hearted. From the moment any real threat to their profits should arise, capitalists would withdraw their investments in panic, credit would be disrupted, factories would close, and a major business crisis would follow. The economic collapse and ensuing chaos can be counted upon to dampen the revolutionary ardor of those workers who cannot see beyond the immediate result of growing poverty, unemployment, and bloodshed.

And bloodshed there will be. For those workers who are not content with whatever share of the growing productivity of industry and agriculture they can wrest from the capitalists in the competitive struggle over wages and working conditions, but who instead insist that the whole social product, and with it bourgeois property, must be in the hands of the working class—they will be in for a fight! One can be sure that the magnates of capital will not be standing around, feuding among themselves, while their graves are being dug. In the name of law and order, property and prosperity, the full force of the oppressive state machinery will be brought to bear on the revolutionaries.

THE ECONOMIC SCENARIO

To achieve victory the revolutionaries must have more than justice on their side. In addition to their own strength, there must be weaknesses in the capitalist economic structure that they can exploit at some opportune moment in history. Much of Marx's work was aimed at uncovering and examining the economic laws that would reveal the causes of capitalist crisis and breakdown and would also point to the opportunities for successful revolutionary action.

The reconstruction of Marx's economic views is a hazardous venture at best, since nowhere does he pull the many strands of his work together into a clear, concise analysis. At the very least, his theories on the economic demise of capitalism must be separated into two parts: (1) the long-run tendency toward capitalist breakdown through the fall in the rate of profit; and (2) the ever-deepening series of cyclical crises which hamper the development of productive forces and encourage the workers' revolt. For technical and theoretical reasons, the hoped-for secular fall in the rate of profit did not materialize. We shall therefore confine our discussion here to Marx's theory of cyclical crises.

According to Keynes, since the days when Malthus unsuccessfully grappled with it, the problem of effective demand "could only live on furtively, below the surface, in the underworlds of Karl Marx, Silvio Gesell or Major Douglas."[16] Well, it depends on one's point of view as to who is above and who is below the surface. If Marx did not ripple the placid pool of neoclassical theory, perhaps that was because it was well submerged beneath the turbulent sea of industry and finance.

Years before Keynes was born, Marx had subjected Say's Law, and—what amounts to the same thing—Ricardo's denial of the possibility of overproduction, to withering criticism. He showed that the abstract possibility of crisis could be found in the very essence of capitalist production.

Capitalism is a pervasive system of commodity production in which products are produced for exchange. They are first exchanged for money. Then, the proceeds from their sale are saved, invested as capital, or used to purchase consumers' goods and services. Money which is saved can enter into the credit system to be lent in turn to others for investment and consumption. While ultimately there is a unity between purchase and sale, between production and consumption, the indirect route over which transactions are carried out means that they are not immediately equated. The rub lies in the fact that even though both sides of the equation—sale and purchase, production and consumption—are united, each is arrived at independently. It would be a coincidence if purchase and sale matched up at any particular point in time.

If purchase and sale get too far out of line, their unity will reassert itself as a destructive process. "Thus the crisis manifests the unity of the two phases that have become independent of each other."[17]

Abstract Forms of Crisis

Thus separation of sale and purchase creates the abstract framework for crisis. Brilliant though this analysis was, Marx did not believe that one could explain crisis merely by demonstrating the abstract possibility of crisis.

The role of money in separating the two phases (purchase and sale) of commodity exchange puts the crisis into slightly more concrete terms. Marx pointed out that the chain of mutual claims and obligations created a means "through which the possibility [of crisis] can develop into actuality":

> The spinner cannot pay because the weaver cannot pay, neither of them pay the machine manufacture, and the latter does not pay the iron, timber, or coal supplier. And all of these in turn, as they cannot realise the value of their commodities, cannot replace that portion of value which is to replace their constant capital. Thus the general crisis comes into being.[18]

Marx realized that this demonstration of the possibility of crises of circulation was not concrete enough. Money circulated as a means of payment long before there was capitalist production and crises. Some more concrete explanation had to be found for "why their crucial aspect becomes prominent and why the potential contradiction contained in them becomes a real contradiction."[19]

Intermediate Forms of Crisis

Now let us move on from these rather abstract forms of crisis to more concrete, intermediate forms.

First, there can be a raw-materials crisis. A crisis can be touched off by a sharp rise in the price, or shortage of raw materials. A cotton famine in Marx's day, or a petroleum shortage in our own, brought on by a bad harvest, war, or by the machinations of an international cartel, can force production cutbacks, throw workers out on the street, and send a wave of disruption through the entire economy.

Next in the order of crises is the crisis of disproportion. A number of types of disproportion can occur in a capitalist economy: (1) a disproportion between the output of industry and the supply of raw materials; (2) a disproportion between the various branches of industry; (3) a disproportion between the capital goods sector and the consumer goods sector owing to uneven depreciation, and renewal, of fixed capital; or (4) a disproportion between the sphere of production and that of circulation or credit. In any case, their equalization may be brought about through a crisis by which capital is transferred from one branch of the economy to another. The effect is similar to that of a raw-materials crisis, only it is caused not by a cut-off in supplies, but by the uneven development of various branches of production. Should the use of electricity, for example, grow much faster than the output of coal mining, or the construction of railroad cars and barges needed to haul it, that could result in induced shortages and a series of cutbacks in industry. Although the effects of either of these two forms of crisis—the raw-materials crisis or the crisis of disproportion—may be severe and widespread, neither one is the result of the type of fundamental contradiction that would doom the capitalist system.

A still more concrete and inescapable form of crisis is the crisis of overproduction-underconsumption. This is the form of crisis outlined in *The Communist Manifesto*. We know that under capitalism, workers must always produce more than they consume. "They must always be *over-producers,* produce over and above their needs."[20] Otherwise there would be no profit (including interest) or rent.

Unless the difference is made up by the consumption and investments of capitalists and landlords, the classical identity between production and consumption (as expressed in Say's Law) will break down, and a general crisis will ensue.

The danger of an overproduction-underconsumption crisis is ever-present. The force which creates it is continually at work. What exactly is this force? Competition! The same competition which was Adam Smith's "invisible hand" of regulation and harmony was for Karl Marx the left hand overturning and disrupting the productive balance. The capitalist must continuously struggle to maintain his market position and his mastery over the workers. He is forced to continually expand output by investing in new cost-cutting and labor-saving technics. This expanding output requires an expanding market to absorb it. But the rise in wages, which might enable workers to buy the additional goods, is held down by the competition between workers for available jobs and the subordination of worker to capitalist, of workman to machine. These opposing facets of the competitive process, the expansion of production and the depression of wages, create a tension which always threatens to build into a crisis of overproduction-underconsumption:

> The ultimate reason for all real crises always remains the poverty and restricted consumption of the masses as opposed to the drive of capitalist production to develop the productive forces as though only the absolute consuming power of society constituted their limit.[21]

Thus when production and consumption (supply and demand) get too far out of line, capitalists can no longer sell all of their products. A crisis takes place. Prices fall, production is cut, workers are fired.

But firing workers only aggravates the crisis, since that means that less wages will be paid and, as a result, there will be still less demand for the products which industry can turn out. That leads to another round of cutbacks, still more unemployment, and so on. It seems as though the process can never end.

Yet it does. Somehow production, which had been rising faster than consumption during prosperity, now falls faster than consumption during a crisis. Prices have dropped, meaning that more goods can be bought with less money. Foreign markets may have been less affected by the crisis than the domestic market. And most important of all, perhaps, the value of capital has been depreciated because its earning power is now less. That means that the capitalists have taken a loss on their investments, but it also means that it will be easier to show a profit, now that the total value of their investment is less. Once the downward spiral has continued until excessive stocks are dried up and capital is sufficiently depreciated, the process of capital accumulation begins anew.

The Industrial Reserve Army

Our discussion of these intermediate forms of crisis still leaves out a crucial element of social tension and cyclical decay, which Marx discovered through his criticism of the law of population. Marx agreed with the classical view that the increase in laborers created a tendency for wages to be reduced to a subsistence minimum. But just as he sought the limit to accumulation within the process of capitalist production itself, not in an external barrier of nature, so did he look for his law of population in the inner workings of capitalist society rather than in some natural biological propensity.

In the long run, the growth of capital means increasing numbers of workers. "Accumulation of capital is," wrote Marx, "increase of the proletariat."[22] As capital expands, the demand for labor increases and wages should improve. But this only means that the "golden chain" the wage worker has forged for himself is allowed to slacken a bit. In time, the growth in the labor force will increase the competition for jobs, allowing industry to tighten its grip over wages once again.

Does that still sound a lot like the dismal Malthusian Law? Yes, but with Marx it was only a tendency, not an iron law. As we said before, Marx did not see a natural limit to output—either industrial or agricultural. He also ridiculed the classical notion that variations in the absolute number of the working population could be tied to the periodic expansions and contractions of capital. Since industry was on a decennial cycle of boom and bust, it would be a neat trick indeed if the size of the working population could fluctuate in step with the demands of industry!

The law of population Marx discovered was specific to the capitalist mode of production. This was the law of "relative surplus-population" or, to use Marx's more picturesque term, the law of the creation of an "industrial reserve army."

Here is how the law works. As new production techniques are introduced and productivity of labor increases, labor power is constantly becoming redundant. Thus, the advancing technics of capital produce an ever-growing surplus population or reserve army of the unemployed.[23] The creation of the reserve army in turn serves as the lever for further accumulation: the competition for jobs by the unemployed keeps the level of wages in check; further, the unemployed form a pool of labor from which the workers for new industries are drawn—as for the railways, in Marx's day.

Thus the effects of Marx's Law of Surplus-Population are quite different from those of the classical theory of population. Both laws serve to oppress the laborer and push his standard of living down to a low level. In the classical law, for which political economy earned the name of "the dismal science," the inexorable increase in numbers, pressing against a limited resource base, condemned the laborer to poverty. Marx believed that there was no limit to expansion, that instead wages are held in check through the laws of supply and demand for labor itself, but not necessarily at a subsistence minimum.

Concrete, Periodic Crisis of Capital

Armed with the notion of the industrial reserve army, we can now attack the concrete causes of capitalist crisis. Its highest expression is to be found in Marx's analysis of "The General Law of Capitalist Accumulation" (*Capital*, Volume 1, Chapter 25). Let us trace his description of the process by which crises inevitably arise.[24]

As the capital of a nation grows, the number of workers employed grows also. The increasing number of machines being built and used, and the growing volume of raw materials being processed, outstrip the growth of labor productivity, summoning up a demand for more labor. Unemployment falls (the industrial reserve army shrinks), forcing capitalists to compete more intensely for workers, driving up wages. If wages rise too fast, the profit rate will fall, both blunting the stimulus and reducing the funds for further investment.

The twin obstacles of high wages and low profits precipitate a crisis. The overall rate of accumulation slows, although the introduction of labor-saving inventions may be speeded up. Workers are thrown out on the street. As the reserve army of unemployed swells its ranks, the competition among workers for jobs grows more intense. Wages drop and capital's dominance over labor is restored.

Through this mechanism of crisis, the obstacles that were created during the expansion phase are removed and capital accumulation can begin anew.

Seen in this light, unemployment is not a side effect of capitalist accumulation or the result of a temporary imbalance in the system. The creation of a relative surplus population is at the very heart of the accumulation process—it is the mechanism by which capitalist exploitation is preserved:

> The rise of wages . . . is confined within limits that not only leave intact the foundations of the capitalist system, but also secure its reproduction on a progressive scale.[25]

In essence, the periodic crises of industry boil down to the shifting balance of power between capital and labor. As the productivity of labor grows, a stream of workers is continuously "set free" by capital to join the ranks of the reserve army, and wages are held in check. If the process of capital accumulation proceeds so fast that the labor reserve is thinned, the advance in wages will cut into the accustomed profits of manufacture, and a crisis will set in to restore the despotism of capital. Hence, the size of the industrial reserve corresponds inversely to the periodic changes of the industrial cycle. The function of the industrial cycle is to keep the pretensions of labor in check.

In explaining how the rate of profit is determined, Marx succinctly summed up that it "resolves itself into a question of the respective powers of the combatants."[26] He added that the constant creation of labor redundance is an essential weapon in the capitalists' arsenal.

Now we have a picture of Marx's concrete periodic crisis of capital, complete with its cycle of unemployment.[27] But does this explanation of economic crisis jive with the less developed forms we spoke of earlier, especially the overproduction-underconsumption crisis? No, not really. In fact, the growing demand for labor that shifts the balance in favor of the workers and brings about the crisis just described has a countereffect on the crisis of overproduction-underconsumption. In Keynesian terms, the shift from profits to wages has the effect of raising the overall propensity to consume, thus narrowing the gap between the demand for commodities and their supply. Conversely, the growing output of goods and services, for which a market must be found if there is to be no crisis of overproduction, is the very means by which the rise in labor's demands can be met, at least partially, without disturbing the proportion between wages and profits.

If we look at the two forms of crisis more abstractly, perhaps we can see more clearly how they conflict. The overproduction-under-consumption crisis is brought about by too little demand for commodities (machinery, raw materials, services, and consumer's products); the concrete periodic crisis we just developed is caused by too much demand for one commodity: labor. Higher wages for labor in the latter form of crisis would indirectly help to supply the missing demand for commodities which brought on the overproduction-underconsumption crisis.[28]

While these two forms of crisis counteract one another, we must not suppose for one moment that they cancel each other out. We cannot presume to have demonstrated an absolute contradiction in Marx's analysis, or have shown, using his very own theories of crisis, that capitalism is an essentially harmonious system. We have not shown that crises are merely the means by which the inevitable disproportions of a dynamic, growing system of production and distribution are corrected.

Although these are counteracting forms of crisis, the basic tensions of capitalism cannot be reconciled in this way. Not only can capitalism never be a system of full employment, it is precisely a period of rising wages (and employment) that immediately precedes the inevitable collapse.[29] Marx showed that full employment is anathema to equilibrium. Clearly he believed that crises and unemployment are the essential means by which the power of the capitalist class is maintained.[30]

Keynes seemed to understand this point instinctively, even though he rejected this explanation of its cause:

> The economic system in which we live . . . seems capable of remaining in a chronic condition of sub-normal activity for a considerable period without any marked tendency either towards recovery or towards complete collapse. Moreover, the evidence indicates that full, or even approximately full, employment is of rare and short-lived occurrence.[31]

The mere fact, therefore, that except during brief periods of specu-lative excess there is a chronic underemployment of the resources available to capital, does not mean that capitalism is in a permanent state of crisis. Rather, full employment is itself a phase of crisis—an unstable state that consists of a temporary erosion of the power of capital. For Marx, "equilibrium" is found not in full employment, but in a fluctuating level of unemployment. But while it is true that he portrays capitalism to be an unstable system, his own theories include a powerful stabilizing mechanism not found in either the classical or the Keynesian analyses: the reserve army of the unemployed.[32]

At first glance any sort of crisis appears to feed upon itself in such a way as to render it virtually impossible to maintain any sort of stability in the system. A second look reveals built-in regenerative processes which diminish the inescapable character of crises. We saw this in the intermediate overproduction-underconsumption crisis in Marx, and in his more concrete crisis, centered around capital accumulation and the growth of the industrial reserve army. Both have built-in regenerative factors which restore stability and establish the foundation from which a new, higher level of output is reached. Add to this the fact that the two types of cycles counteract one another, and we might be led to conclude that capitalism is inherently a system of frequent, albeit not necessarily severe, ups and downs.

Marx's theories indicate that though capitalism is based upon chronic unemployment, business crises arising from the process of capital accumulation take on the appearance of cyclical ups and downs rather than that of a continuous degenerative spiral. The road would be bumpy and the social relations of capitalism could keep the economy from its full growth potential, but competition insures the improvement of productive techniques and expansion of output.

We can conclude our discussion of the economic scenario by noting that it is one thing to demonstrate the necessity for cyclical crises of capitalism, quite another to prove the inevitability of capitalism's final crisis or death.

Cyclical crisis can be deduced from the free competition, or struggle, between capital and labor together with the drive for continual expansion of the scale of production. Without the introduction of some compelling technical barrier, it is difficult to predict capitalism's demise from the economic scenario alone.

COMBINING AND SUMMARIZING

Although it is useful to abstract the purely economic crisis from its actual social-political setting, we must not lose sight of the need to return to the concrete institutional framework before Marx's theory of the process of capitalist breakdown and socialist transformation can be thoroughly understood. As we said at the beginning, there is no evidence to suggest that Marx believed that economic crisis alone would bring about the downfall of capital. As he and Engels wrote in *The Communist Manifesto*:

> [N]ot only has the bourgeoisie forged the weapons that bring death to itself; it has also called into existence the men who are to wield those weapons—the modern working class—the proletarians.[33]

Marx also wrote that the law of capital accumulation (which creates the industrial reserve army) "rivets the laborer to capital more firmly than the wedges of Vulcan did Prometheus to the rock. It establishes an accumulation of misery, corresponding with accumulation of capital."[34] The tyranny of capital would not, Marx believed, cease on its own accord. It was the historic mission of the proletariat to organize to smash the wages system—to abolish the mode of production "in which the laborer exists to satisfy the needs of self-expansion of existing values, instead of, on the contrary, material wealth existing to satisfy the needs of development on the part of the laborer."[35]

In this context, it is important to again point out that in Marx's social-political scenario for the downfall of capital, the individual hedonism of classical political economy is displaced by enlightened class consciousness. The working class must break the laws of supply and demand which hold all workers down by keeping them in competition with one another. They must go beyond their immediate interests of higher wages, shorter hours, and improved working conditions to abolish the wages system itself:

> They ought to understand that, with all the miseries it imposes upon them, the present system simultaneously engenders the *material conditions* and the *social forms* necessary for an economic reconstruction of society. Instead of the *conservative* motto: "*A fair day's wages for a fair day's work!*" they ought to inscribe on their banner the *revolutionary* watchword: "*Abolition of the wages system!*"[36]

This short passage goes to the heart of the dilemma. There can be a big difference between what the working class *ought* to do and what it *will* do. Capitalist accumulation establishes the material foundation for improving the workers' standard of living. But the actual attainment of an improved level of living, whether through class struggle or through the laws of supply and demand, might serve to dampen the revolutionary fires and even help to maintain the balance between production and consumption upon which the health of capitalism depends.

And so, the very creation of the actual instrument for the overthrow of the capitalist order—the organized proletariat—inasmuch as it achieves its demands for a greater share of the social product and an improvement in working conditions, has the salubrious effect of closing the gap between production and demand. The very process of dissolution, when stood on its head, becomes a force for renewing the vigor of expansion and accumulation.

From a present-day perspective, Marx's scenarios also have a technological hitch. In the United States today, the irrationality of the capitalist system is more than the anarchy of rival capitals and competing class interests. Many of the contradictions of advanced capitalism are not resoluble along class lines, even if the transcendence of capitalist society is one prerequisite to their solution. In terms of the ties between man and nature, or of the unity between private means and social ends, each advance of industry along the principle of optimum net gain makes it more difficult to achieve future industrial rationality and organic balance. For example, when the French Communist trade unions lobby for the production of Concorde supersonic airliners, they are, without being aware of it perhaps, making a tradeoff between immediate goals and long-term organic need.

In essence, Marx attacked the classical ideal on its own ground, by mercilessly exposing the class conflicts and economic tensions inherent in the competitive system. By positing capitalist expansion as the springboard to a socialist future, he also put himself in the seemingly inescapable dilemma of proving capital's failure by its success.

Considering the great strides capital has since taken, Marx's scenarios for its downfall are, by themselves, rather unconvincing. What is more crucial, Marx basically does not question the industrial imperatives of the competitive order. His theories cannot, in themselves, comprehend the full complexity of capitalist decay.

1987528

Part 2
THE PERILS
OF PROGRESS

Capital has proven to be a mighty force. Is it also a rational, self-sustaining mechanism? That depends on both the correctness and inclusiveness of the classical competitive model, a hypothetical ideal much celebrated but little criticized.

Certainly a rational or self-sustaining mechanism may mean different things in different times or from different perspectives. Traditionally, capitalist rationality has been construed in the sense of a continuous industrial progress which underwrites national grandeur and pays out material dividends to investors and workers alike. Yet even from this limited frame of reference, certain underlying assumptions, or postulates, are required for the competitive model to hold up in the long run. Briefly, these are:

1. Natural resources are unlimited;
2. Capital can dominate nature;
3. The interests of the individual and society are one;
4. Capitalism is based on rational motive;
5. Competitive vitality continues over time;
6. There is a separation of economic and political power.

The next six chapters are devoted to an in-depth analysis of the postulates. It will be seen that the balanced harmony of classical political economy now rests on a faltering foundation.

4

The Destruction of Resources

Après nous le déluge!

Anonymous

Capitalism devours material resources.

The production of goods under capitalism is a process which takes resources—land, minerals, and fuel—and transforms them, using human labor and machines, into marketable commodities. This process is now being carried out on an unprecedented scale. To illustrate, here is a list of the raw materials used up *annually* for every man, woman, and child in the United States: 20,550 pounds of nonmetal resources (such as sand, stone, gravel, cement, and phosphate), 1,200 pounds of iron and steel, 50 pounds of aluminum, 25 pounds of copper, 15 pounds of zinc, 15 pounds of lead, 25 pounds of other metals, plus—mainly for fuel—7,800 pounds of petroleum, 5,000 pounds of coal, 5,000 pounds of natural gas, and 1/20 pound of uranium.[1] Nor should we overlook the vast quantities of renewable, but strictly limited, reserves of land and water used by farms, factories, and households. When 87 billion gallons of fresh water are used every day, it too is on its way to becoming a precious resource.[2]

Considering the rate at which resources are now being used, large reserves will be needed for the future. Yet there is no mechanism, either according to classical theory or through the everyday operation of business, by which resources are harbored. There are no means by which present-day production takes future needs into consideration.

True, prices for raw materials will rise as supplies run out, thereby restricting their use. But that type of regulation, particularly in a competitive market, is notoriously after the fact:

In spite of expanding demands for minerals and materials, prices in constant dollars have not changed much over the past 15 years, with the exception of petroleum and some metals. Prices of some commodities have even declined or have fluctuated both above and below the norm.[3]

Stated crudely, a capitalist system operates on the basis that natural resources are unlimited. Unlimited not in the sense that there is no price for them—but in that it is not necessary to anticipate future resource needs. Capital does not adjust present-day production on consideration of the future availability of resources.[4]

Most economists even today believe that the problem of limited resources is not theoretically important. In their view, capitalist economics has "solved" the problem of production and they see no limit to future growth and prosperity. Thus, such an eminently sensible man as Bernard D. Nossiter recently wrote:

We do know how to order a modern, industrialized economy so that it maintains a high level of employment and an ever-increasing flow of goods and services. Any skeptic should consult the more or less unbroken wave of prosperity since the end of the Second World War.[5]

Such reaffirmations of faith are in keeping with the prevailing belief in everlasting classical harmony. Few economists paused to reflect that "ever-increasing" production involves physical processes which drain and disrupt the earth's mineral and biological reserves.

From the time of its inception, capitalist production has been drawing down the stock of mineral and biological capital. For example, mining, the most important industry in the development of modern capitalism, devoured an endless amount of wood for timbers, machines, and the smelting of metals:

By the seventeenth century the marvelous oak forests of England had already been sacrificed to the iron-maker: so serious was the shortage that the Admiralty under Sir John Evelyn was forced to pursue a vigorous policy of reforestation in order to have enough timber for the Royal Navy.[6]

By ignoring the resource question, the competitive economic model merely reflects the prevailing mode of production under study. Then, too, populations were much smaller than those of today, and the rapacious powers of technology were comparatively primitive. There were limitless lands to colonize and frontiers to open up. When the United States had only three million people living on the eastern seaboard, there was no need to worry about future shortages of resources. There was plenty to be found "out West." And even if there was always a price to be paid for resources, a cost in obtaining them, the pioneering entrepreneurs saw no cause to be concerned with the effect of current resource use on future supplies. As an example of that outlook:

> Duluth papers at the turn of the century are filled with braggadocio about the "inexhaustible forests" [of Minnesota]. Yet in about thirty-five years Paul Bunyan's legions had scalped the 40,000 or more square miles of prime pine as clearly as though the great Bunyan ax had been a razor.[7]

This and countless other illustrations of the prodigal nature of capitalist production have failed to impinge themselves on the minds of economists. Their theories reflect the culture and logic of western capitalism which is geared to fighting limitations and working within them. It is not difficult to see why the concept of the "frontier" has played an important role in a culture geared to mechanized plunder:

> As we conclude despoilation of the land we regale ourselves with the promise and potential of the seas. This is what the frontier has always meant to us—an escape from consequences.[8]

Some plunged to new frontiers, others took wing. In what can be described as a flight of fancy, Joseph Schumpeter wrote:

> The conquest of the air may well be more important than the conquest of India was—we must not confuse geographical frontiers with economic ones.[9]

Naturally as the frontiers become closed, capitalists will have to redirect their profit-seeking activities. But that is begging the question. The "conquest of the air" is dependent upon earthbound resources that have been frittered away in geographical exploits. Not only is the world finite, it is shrinking.

This is not to imply that the destruction of resources is an invention of capitalist culture. Since the dawn of civilization, the human race has been cutting away the life-sustaining ground it stands upon:

> Earth's soil mantle has been forming for 350,000,000 years. . . . It kept building up until 6,000 B.C., when man first devised a cultivating implement and dropped a few seeds into holes, thus initiating the

agricultural era. From that moment, the soil mantle has been (literally) "going downhill." In all parts of the globe not under the polar icecaps, many inches of topsoil have been lost to erosion; in richest sections the erosion is counted in feet, not inches. It is difficult to believe that the bared mountains of Italy, Syria, Lebanon, and even the Armenian hills were once thickly forested slopes.[10]

Now the earth's resources are being plundered at an unprecedented rate. In the year 1870 there were 48 acres of land available for every man, woman, and child in the United States. Since then, environmental abuse, population growth, urban sprawl, and the automobile have cut this figure to 10.6 acres per person, only 2.6 of them suitable for cultivated crops.[11] Since 1940 industry has consumed more primary metal than during the whole of previous history.[12] And the table on page 44—which shows the estimated ratio of resource reserves to anticipated world demand between now and the year 2000—indicates that serious shortages are on the horizon.

A resource/demand ratio of less than 1.0 indicates that recoverable reserves at current costs will be exceeded by world demand before the turn of the century. By this measure, supplies of copper, gold, lead, mercury, natural gas, petroleum, silver, tin, tungsten, and zinc will all have run out. If all countries consumed raw material at the same rate as the United States, every resource on the list but coal, iron, and platinum would be exhausted within the next three decades.

Of course, the figures in this table reflect only known reserves, worth recovering at present prices using current techniques. These are, for now, the economically exploitable reserves—they certainly do not reflect the total quantities of these minerals available in the earth's crust. It is reasonable to assume that further prospecting, new extraction techniques, and higher raw-material prices will considerably swell the volume of commercially usable resource reserves, and that increased recycling will help to hold down demand.

Still, considering the rate at which the earth's resources are being devoured, it is clear that the expanding industrial and agricultural demands will not be satisfied much longer. From the cradle to maturity, capitalism has relied on limitless resources to feed its growing appetites. That era of the open frontier is approaching its end. This is the hard truth behind the seemingly commonplace observance by the Council on Environmental Quality that "it now appears that the combination of increasing world demands, higher costs of

WORLD DEMAND FOR NONRENEWABLE
RESOURCES, 1971–2000

Resource	Units	World Resource Demand	Resources Recoverable*	Ratio of Resources to Demand
Aluminum	Million Short Tons	1,050	2,468	2.4
Chromium	Million Short Tons	95	132	1.4
Coal				
Anthracite	Million Short Tons	4,707	4,700	1.0
Soft	Billion Short Tons	110	**	10.0+
Cobalt	Million Pounds	2,380	5,460	2.3
Copper	Million Short Tons	393	340	0.9
Gold	Million Troy Ounces	1,374	1,000	0.7
Iron	Billion Short Tons	20	97	4.9
Lead	Million Short Tons	148	57	0.4
Manganese	Million Short Tons	429	577	1.3
Mercury	Thousand Flasks	10,180	3,640	0.4
Molybdenum	Billion Pounds	9	12	1.3
Natural gas	Trillion Cubic Feet	2,611	1,169	0.4
Nickel	Billion Pounds	52	92	1.8
Petroleum	Billion Barrels	1,040	632	0.6
Platinum	Million Troy Ounces	104	357	3.4
Silver	Million Troy Ounces	16,400	5,450	0.3
Tin	Thousand Long Tons	8,480	4,181	0.5
Tungsten	Million Pounds	3,530	2,750	0.8
Zinc	Million Short Tons	250	131	0.5

Source: U. S. Department of Interior, *The Fifth Annual Report of the Council on Environmental Quality*, pp. 308–311.

*Recoverable at US 1971 prices.

**Adequate

fuels, and lower grades of reserves is beginning to overtax supplies and increase prices to a greater degree than heretofore."

Even if the resource estimates cited above are off by a wide margin, it is clear that future production—not to mention its expansion—will have a limited, even shrinking, volume of materials to work with.

But before we proceed further, some account must be taken of the argument that the world's resource problems will be solved by technology. Is it possible that new raw materials will be created and new sources of food and energy will be developed that will allow population and industrial growth to continue unabated for the foreseeable future?

Just a few years ago most people believed that technical progress would or could provide for unlimited growth. Now this unquestioned, almost religious faith is giving way to doubt in the system's ability to provide the good life for all.

That the march of material progress will halt or reverse itself is not just rejected by capitalist ideology, but is an idea completely foreign to it. Capitalism is a system of expansion par excellence. "Accumulate, accumulate! That is the Moses and the prophets!" These words of Marx speak for the very soul of capital. Mill's belief, which we will come to later, that the end of economic growth would not necessarily mean an end to moral and social progress, may have been coolly received one hundred years ago. Today it is met with frozen hostility from business, labor, and government leaders. Without continuous expansion, the incentive of business enterprise is jeopardized. That in turn threatens a bitter feud over what will be produced and who will get it. When the market system runs out of resources, technology is put forth as the solution to continued growth—since the pie must grow, if only for the sake of capitalism's stability.

Since the world is on a deliberate course to continue present patterns of increasing resource use in the belief that technology will solve or circumvent arising shortages, the burden of proof in pursuing such a risky course should certainly lie with the technocrats. Yet such constraints on industrial enterprise that would be engendered by strict conservation policies are so abhorrent that no defense of the status quo is required—even though the current plunderous course increasingly appears destined to folly.

For there appear to be a number of reasons to believe that technology will not yield final solutions to the resource problem. This is especially true of the immediate task of sustaining growth of world food output. Here the long-run prospects do not appear to be good. As industry and population grow, the amount of land available for crops shrinks. And the capitalist era has given birth, literally, to a population growth that has been as unrelenting as its industrial expansion.

The statistics are familiar enough. It was not until 1830 that the population of the world reached one billion. Before the next hundred years were out, in 1930, it had passed the two billion mark. In 1960 there were three billion mouths to feed. In 1976, four billion. The year 2000 . . . ? Five billion would be a modest estimate. The countries of advanced capitalism do not exhibit runaway population growth or face drastic food shortages. But the stability and growth of capitalism as a world system is certainly threatened by the poverty of many of the countries of Asia, Africa, and Latin America.

It is likely that spreading urbanization and the increasing availability and acceptance of birth control will cause an eventual leveling off of world population, but not in time to prevent desperate shortages. Since 1970 there has been a slight downturn in population growth. Birth rates dropped significantly in North America and Western Europe, dramatically in China. There has also been a tragic increase in hunger-related deaths in many of the world's poorer countries.[13]

Until the population level stabilizes, how will the increasing numbers be fed? Large, sparsely populated regions still remain on the globe, but these areas do not hold the same promise for agricultural expansion that Australia or America did a century or two ago. In theory, the Sahara can be made to bloom. But the cost of generating the necessary energy, desalting enough sea water, constructing aqueducts, and producing and transporting the required quantities of fertilizer are prohibitive. Not to mention that no one has yet solved such technical problems as that of how to dispose of the gigantic quantities of salt that would be produced when the sea water is distilled.[14]

If deserts hold little promise, what of the sparsely populated, verdant tropics? Are they the beckoning new frontier? Here is what the geographer S. R. Eyre found when he explored this region:

> At first glance . . . suggestions regarding the potential productivity of the Amazon and Congo basins, Borneo, and the coastlands of New Guinea are more beguiling: these, after all, are well-watered tropical areas with high temperatures throughout the year.
>
> A review of the present man/land ratio in Indonesia puts this problem in a proper perspective. . . . [For example, m]ost of Borneo's soils . . . are on older sedimentary rocks; the igneous rocks that are to be found there are of the rhyolite and dacite groups—base-deficient and inherently infertile. In an area with around 100 inches mean annual precipitation and no dry season, there must also be very rapid leaching. In other words, the agricultural potential of Borneo is very similar to that found over much of the Amazon and Congo Basins and many other smaller areas in the humid tropics which remain sparsely populated. In such areas the clay-humus complex is often less than 5 percent base-saturated as compared to the 70 percent required for a moderately productive soil.[15]

Unless tropical forest cultivation is confined to small clearings, there is a great danger of erosion.[16] And in order to bring modern agricultural practices to these soils, such huge quantities of fertilizer would have to be applied that the cost would be prohibitive for an industrially advanced nation, let alone an impoverished, under-developed one.[17]

As it is, the rising cost of fertilizer is threatening the "green revolution" in Latin America, Africa, and Asia. Increased produc-tion from the new, high-yielding strains of wheat, rice, corn, and other crops is dependent on the use of chemical fertilizers (and insecticides), and the underdeveloped countries are the ones hardest hit by their high costs of production and transportation. The United States consumes 17.7 million tons of fertilizer annually while India, with the same cropland and a much larger population to feed, con-sumed (before recent shortages) a mere 2.9 million tons.[18] As the press pointed out, this is approximately the same amount that is used on American lawns, gardens, golf courses, and cemeteries.[19]

There is room for a considerable increase in world fertilizer output but supplies are ultimately limited, particularly for phosphates. De-posits of this vital mineral appear to be quite restricted—90 percent of world production has come from the US, the USSR, Morocco, and Tunisia.[20] It is difficult to see when the underdeveloped countries will ever receive sufficient supplies of this expensive resource. The energy crisis and the exhaustion of reserves have, in fact, caused fertilizer prices to more than double. India's supplies have dropped from three million tons to two.[21]

But is there some other way that the world can escape food shortages? As the population grows and the amount of cropland shrinks, many have looked toward the vast oceans as a potential-ly inexhaustible source of food. But here too the potential for ex-panding food output is much more limited than would appear at first sight.

To begin with, only the surface waters, where photosynthesis can take place, have food potential. What is not generally appreciated is the fact that most of the vast expanse of the seas is completely unproductive. According to a study by John H. Ryther:

> The open sea—90 per cent of the ocean and nearly three-fourths of the earth's surface—is essentially a biological desert. It produces a negligible fraction of the world's fish catch at present and has little or no potential for yielding more in the future.[22]

ESTIMATED PRODUCTIVITY OF
THE OCEAN BY REGION

Region	Percent of Ocean	Area (km^2)	Primary Production [tons (organic carbon)]	Food Chain Levels	Efficiency of Conversion (percent)	Fish Production (million tons)
Open ocean	90.0	326 × 10^6	16.3 × 10^9	5	10	1.6
Coastal zone*	9.9	36 × 10^6	3.6 × 10^9	3	15	120
Upwelling areas	0.1	3.6 × 10^5	0.1 × 10^9	1 1/2	20	120

Source: Ryther, "Photosynthesis and Fish Production," in *Global Ecology*, pp. 32–33.
*Includes offshore areas of high productivity

The reason for this anomaly can be seen in the following table. In the open ocean, which is not very productive to begin with, there is a long food chain that must be passed through before simple photosynthetic organisms can be converted into human food. In the richer coastal and upwelling regions, the food chain is short and the efficiency of conversion, pound for pound from one food chain level to the next, is much higher. That is to say, in the coastal and upwelling regions, far less energy and matter are "wasted" between photosynthesis and the dinner table. When all these factors are multiplied, it turns out that 10 percent of the ocean produces virtually 100 percent of the fish.

These estimates of the maximum food potential of the world's waters explicitly ignore the continued destruction of inland waters and coastal breeding grounds, and the rising levels of biocides and industrial pollutants in surface waters. Even so, the estimates show that the potential for increased harvests from the seas is strictly limited. Although it is difficult to measure the food potential of the oceans with much precision, S. R. Eyre found that two independent approaches, in line with Ryther's, yielded very similar estimates:

> A summation of the productivity of the upper trophic levels of marine life has produced answers [to the question of the total productivity of the earth's water bodies] of between 300 and 320 m.m.t. [million metric tons] per annum, of which no more than half—150–160 m.m.t. —are harvestable at a sustained yield. When we recollect that the total world catch of aquatic products in 1966 was already in the vicinity of 60 m.m.t., it becomes patently obvious that here is no limitless supply.[23]

Already it appears that most of the world's major fisheries are being harvested at near—or, as in the case of the continental shelf, even beyond—the maximum sustainable yield. Ryther concluded that:

Much of the potential expansion must consist of new products from remote regions, such as the Antarctic Krill, for which no harvesting technology and no market yet exist.[24]

While this examination of the food potential of the earth's lands and waters is admittedly a cursory one, it seems that we can safely draw three conclusions from it:

(1) There is a practical limit to global food production.
(2) As the limit is approached, the law of diminishing returns will dictate that each succeeding incremental output will require an ever-increasing volume of capital—machinery, fertilizer, and energy.
(3) These growing capital inputs have a negative feedback on agricultural output. Industrial expansion uses up land and pollutes the oceans, thereby diminishing the potential food supply still further.

The advanced capitalist nations will not be faced with mass hunger, but we must remember that capitalism is a world system. From its inception, capital has been an international régime of free trade among the rich, and unabashed plunder of the poor. A striking, if grotesque, illustration of how the system continues to work can be found in Pierre Jalée's work *The Third World in World Economy*. He found that between the years 1956 and 1964 food production for local consumption grew little or not at all in Third World countries and actually declined on a per capita basis. But at the very time that these countries were backsliding into hunger, they busily increased their production of agricultural products for export to the developed capitalist economies. Coffee production was up 46 percent; cocoa production, 70 percent. To satisfy western demands they produced 43 percent more cotton and 18 percent more natural rubber.[25]

A specific example can be taken from Brazil, which experienced no significant increase in food production for local consumption over the past decade, while its population increased 20 to 30 percent. Land which used to produce grain for Brazilians now yields ten million tons of soybeans for Japan.[26]

The growing world food shortage threatens this system of market dependency. Less and less can the poor nations afford to absorb the expanding output of industrial products western factories turn out. Their stagnant markets offer fewer and fewer investment opportunities for foreign capital.

Hunger and poverty have only one basic solution. As the Chinese have shown, the answer is not to be found through foreign aid and investment, or the import of expensive western technology. What is the secret? To liberate the vast store of human energy, ability, and discipline that the existing class system either has no use for, or is unable to tap.

The West is afraid of the revolutionary solution—quite rightly. Although part of its fear is hysterical anticommunism, there is the real possibility that foreign markets and investments will be lost or that vital supplies of raw material will be cut off. Imperialists feel more comfortable with an apartheid régime or a Chilean junta.

But let us suppose for a moment that the food shortage could be eliminated through revolutionary developments in the poor nations and that it would not drastically affect the world market of raw materials. What will happen to industrial growth? Can it still go on indefinitely? Or will it grind to a halt as nonfood resources run out?

Here there can be no prima facie case for pessimism concerning the possibilities for technological solutions. Energy and matter, after all, are neither created nor destroyed by industry—they are simply transformed from a less useful into a more useful form. However, the practical evidence is overwhelmingly negative.

As the readily available supplies of nonrenewable natural resources run out, new techniques for extracting, transporting, and refining less accessible and lower-grade reserves of minerals and raw materials tend to be highly capital-intensive and energy-consuming.[27] It is also commonly assumed that although high-grade mineral deposits are being used up, there exist great quantities of reserves of a slightly lower quality; that as the grade of ore decreases arithmetically, the quantity increases geometrically.

Apparently there is much less geological evidence to support this arithmetic-geometric theory of ore deposits than is commonly assumed. Many ore deposits exhibit sharp decreases in quantity as the quality of reserves drops off. Among these are the majority of deposits of mercury, gold, silver, tungsten, lead, zinc, antimony, and beryllium.

> In many important types of mineral deposits, all available evidence indicates a paucity of the low-grade material essential to the concept of the arithmetic-geometric ratios. For lead-zinc replacement deposits in carbonate rocks, this zone is commonly but a few feet wide, and limestone carrying 20 or 30 ppm [parts per million] may be within arm's reach of a huge ore body having a grade ten thousand times that of the countryrock.[28]

This indicates that sooner or later, depending on the rate at which the mining of cheap supplies exceeds new discoveries, the increasing world demand for many raw materials will have to be met with greatly increased inputs of capital, labor, and energy. All the minerals we could conceivably use are there, of course, in the earth's crust. But we must not comfort ourselves with the belief that technology will find a way to unlock nature's treasures:

> Surprisingly enough, many men unfamiliar with the mineral industry believe that the beneficent gods of Technology are about to open the cornucopia of granite and sea, flooding industry with any and all metals desired. Unfortunately cheap energy—[assuming nuclear breeder reactors become a reality]—little reduces the total costs—chiefly made up of capital and labor—required for mining and processing rock. The enormous quantities of unusable waste produced for each unit of metal also are more easily disposed of on a blueprint than in the field.[29]

As was the case with food production, a vicious circle sets in as the additional capital, labor, and energy needed to produce raw materials passes the point of diminishing returns. Eventually, many of the technical "solutions" to one problem or another may destroy more wealth than they create, especially when we consider that new technologies designed to cope with resource shortages often result in stepped-up destruction of the ecosystem and disastrous rises in pollution levels. Not all new technologies are bad, but it would be folly to let the notion of technical progress blind us to the need for judicious conservation.

Considering the present level of the world's industrial production and the tremendous growth in population that has occurred over the past 150 years, the proposition that natural resources are unlimited becomes untenable. If we are to have a manageable economic future, the industrially advanced nations will have to conserve resources very carefully and drastically alter patterns of consumption. This must be done through rational planning and management. But, except for the fact that the price of raw materials increases as supplies run out, the classical competitive market is incapable of carrying out that feat. The free market can never take the future into account. It assumes that we will never run out of what we have—there will always be a cost in obtaining resources, but they will not be any more scarce tomorrow than they are today.

Political economy is founded on the belief that natural resources will always be plentiful. Most economists implicitly endorse this view, but few expressed it as openly as Schumpeter:

Even if, for the sake of argument, we grant that humanity's geographical frontier is closed for good—which is not in itself very obvious in view of the fact that at present there are deserts where once there were fields and populous cities—and even if we further grant that nothing will ever contribute to human *welfare* as much as did the foodstuffs and raw materials from those new lands—which is more plausible— it does not follow that total output per head must therefore decline, or increase at a smaller rate, during the next half-century. . . . Technological progress effectively turned the tables on any such tendency, and it is one of the safest predictions that in the calculable future we shall live in an *embarras de richesses* of both foodstuffs and raw materials, giving all the rein to expansion of total output that we shall know what to do with. This applies to mineral resources as well.[30]

Classical political economy, like the capitalist system it describes, assumes that we live only for the present. The rationality of the market does not extend to providing a future for our children and grandchildren. The moment we let considerations of future welfare affect present economic decisions even if that future is only ten or twenty years hence, it becomes necessary to transcend the classical system by interjecting a system of planned resource use.

The primitive efficiency of the competitive market is no longer enough. Even if government planners could effect a general increase in the prices (above the competitive norm) for those raw materials which need to be conserved, there would still be no distinction as to wasteful or productive use. No distinction would be made, say, as to the use of aluminum for buildings or beer cans.

On a purely national scale, a capitalist government could attempt to correct the short-sightedness of the market by putting quotas on mining and forestry. It could assign user fees and taxes that would promote conservation for various inputs such as water and electricity. It could encourage less wasteful packaging. Wasteful outputs —such as aerosols, beverage cans, and snowmobiles—could be barred. The government could put a one-thousand-dollar "resource tax" on a four-thousand-pound automobile to encourage the production of smaller cars, or no cars at all. There are many ways that the government could intervene in the competitive market to correct the failure to anticipate future resource needs.

But there is a hitch. Even if it were politically possible to implement them, such controls would necessarily be so detailed and pervasive that they would severely constrain or even displace the functioning of the competititve market mechanism itself. All decisions would come from a central government planning agency. Many branches of production would become privately owned, public utilities. There would have to be a dual system of private-public management. Government bureaucrats would make the important decisions regarding what should be produced: the allowable designs, inputs, costs, and selling prices. Even if such policies were possible to effect, they would negate the very system of intricate market checks and balances which they seek to rationalize.

It is clear then that rational resource management is incompatible with the operation of freely competitive markets in the classical sense. But might capitalism come up with a practical solution to this problem which, though not as nice theoretically, would nevertheless result in a somewhat rational use of natural resources? Might the modern business be a better resource-manager than its competitive predecessor? If we accept John Kenneth Galbraith's thesis that giant corporations are rational planners, we might assume the answer is yes.

> The size of General Motors is in the service not of monopoly or the economics of scale but of planning. And for this planning—control of supply, control of demand, provision of capital, minimization of risk—there is no clear upper limit to the desirable size.[31]

Let's extend Galbraith's argument a bit to apply to the problem of resource management. If the "technostructure" of the auto industry could see that the country is running out of petroleum and that the prospects for switching to another source of fuel are not very promising, might General Motors take the initiative to withhold fuel-hungry auto air conditioners from the market, or discourage their use by making them very expensive? They would conserve gasoline now in order to have enough to run their cars in future years. Is this not within the rational (theoretical) functioning of a monopolistic system?

If we assume that the auto industry is perfectly competitive on the other hand, there is absolutely no reason, apart from consumer demand, for the various companies to withhold air conditioning on the basis of conserving future resources. Each company is engaged in a purely day-to-day market battle. It will produce and sell everything it can without regard to the future resource picture—because if it does not produce the air conditioners for cars, another company will, making the first company's cars less competitive.

To take another hypothetical example, suppose one corporation controlled all the forests in the country. Would it be likely to have a plan to survive in the future, in addition to reaping immediate profits? As a monopoly, it would have full control over the forestry resources and the power to decide how they would be expended. Would it not tend to assume planning functions that would not exist in a purely competitive economy? The company might plan its production so that instead of devastating the forests though clear cutting, or cutting down all the hardwood and leaving scrub and soft pine behind, it might control harvesting in order to have profits twenty or forty years in the future. In other words, the company might price future resources and manage them better than if a purely competitive industry existed.

"The corporation," wrote Baran and Sweezy, "is in principle immortal and inculcates in its functionaries a long time horizon."[32] Is it conceivable that a monopoly capitalist system would ravage natural resources less rapidly than its competitive counterpart? Monopolists would achieve higher prices by conserving resources (thus restricting supply), and such a policy might conserve their long-run profits as well.

That sounds logical, but there are several reasons why we cannot conserve resources by encouraging monopoly:

First, the corporate time horizon is still much too short. Corporate plans generally extend only a few years into the future—at best for a decade or two. If civilized human society is to plan its survival for the indefinite future, it will be necessary to draw up resource plans in terms of half centuries or even centuries.

The lumber industry provides a prime example of this failure. Although it is dominated by giant corporations which boast of supposed vast resources, their logging practices are disastrously shortsighted and wasteful. As private reserves run out, the industry steps up its political pressure to "harvest" publicly owned forests.[33]

Second, interindustry product competition reduces the sphere of potential corporate resource management.

Going back to our auto industry example, if air-conditioned public transport is a substitute for private cars, it is likely that General Motors would encourage, rather than discourage, sales of air-conditioned cars. The future benefits from marginal resource conservation would be minor compared to the immediate profit loss resulting from product substitution.

Third, many industries would derive little benefit, even over time, from a policy of reduced resource consumption, since the amount of resources they use are only a fraction of society's total consumption.

There is a great need, for example, to conserve the world's dwindling supplies of copper. Manufacturers of radios and televisions consume significant amounts of copper, yet this probably amounts to only a small percent of the total used by industry. If particular industries hold back on production to conserve copper supplies, they would only be aiding other industries dependent on copper, or their foreign competitors, without making any significant change in their own future resource picture.

Fourth, no industry will voluntarily shut itself down.

The entire automobile industry is a disastrous misappropriation of resources, yet it is doubtful that the auto manufacturers, petroleum companies, service stations, road-builders, garage owners, tire manufacturers, and parts dealers will decide to shut down operations as a gesture of public goodwill.

Aside from the public relations advertising of General Motors, Weyerhauser, and Exxon, there is little evidence to support the view that monopolies promote better resource use than competitive industries. In fact, monopolistic industries frequently use their vast political powers to prevent or overturn public conservation policies. The Alaskan pipeline, strip mining, the cutting down of national forests, and the highway trust fund are but a few of the many examples of monopolistic abuse of resources. Moreover, encouraging monopoly for the purpose of conserving resources would, just as in the case of government control, amount to killing the goose that laid the prosperity egg. It would destroy much of what remains of the capitalist system of competitive market checks and incentives.

There needs to be monopoly control over the utilization and management of resources in the sense of overall social goals and policies. But there is no reason to believe that private monopolies, aside from when they hold down production to prevent "ruinous" competition, are a better means to achieving those ends than the competitive market.

Of our six postulates, the classical economists were most aware of the first: that capitalist expansion was based on the presumption of unlimited natural resources. Adam Smith or David Ricardo, even John Stuart Mill or Karl Marx, would be astounded if he could see the amount of resources used by industry today. Even so, there are limits. On the matter of resource use, theory is finally being overtaken by reality.

5

Ecological Suicide

And God said, Let us make man in our image, after our likeness:
and let them have dominion over the fish of the sea, and over the
fowl of the air, and over the cattle, and over all the earth, and
over every creeping thing that creepeth upon the earth.

Genesis 1:26

The belief that nature is the servant of man is one of the fundamental articles of faith of capitalist culture. The examination of this belief
from the standpoint of political economy, with all its implications
and ramifications, might be termed the study of "bionomics."[1]

And what should the study of bionomics include? A good way to
introduce the subject would be to restate the four laws of ecology:[2]

(1) The First Law of Ecology: *Everything Is Connected to Everything Else*
This law expresses the meaning of the "balance of nature."
All living things exist in complex relations with each other
and their organic environments. Any disruption or imbalance in one part of an ecosystem causes stress upon the entire
system by sending shock waves along the links in the environmental chain. One broken link may even cause the entire
ecological network to collapse.

Productive activities frequently disrupt ecological cycles. Since
DDT has no part in the organic environment, earthworms living in
a cornfield sprayed with a concentration of one unit will achieve a
concentration of from ten to forty units. Woodcocks feeding on the
earthworms will, in turn, have DDT levels of about two hundred

units. A small perturbation in one part of the ecological network may have long-delayed effects which will be large and distant.

(2) The Second Law of Ecology: *Everything Must Go Somewhere*
"In nature," writes Commoner, "there is no such thing as 'waste'. . . . A persistent effort to answer the question 'Where does it go?' can yield a surprising amount of valuable information about an ecosystem. Consider, for example, the fate of a household item which contains mercury—a substance with serious environmental effects that have just recently surfaced. A dry-cell battery containing mercury is purchased, used to the point of exhaustion, and then 'thrown out.' But where does it really go? First, it is placed in a container of rubbish; this is collected and taken to an incinerator. Here the mercury is heated; this produces mercury vapor which is emitted by the incinerator stack, and mercury *vapor* is toxic. Mercury vapor is carried by the wind, eventually brought to earth in rain or snow. Entering a mountain lake, let us say, the mercury condenses and sinks to the bottom. Here it is acted on by bacteria which convert it into methyl mercury. This is soluble and taken up by fish; since it is not metabolized, the mercury accumulates in the organs and flesh of the fish. The fish is caught and eaten by a man and the mercury becomes deposited in his organs, where it might be harmful."[3]

(3) The Third Law of Ecology: *Nature Knows Best*
Natural systems have been carefully built up through millions of years of experimentation through processes known as natural selection. Wherever human productivity intervenes in or changes a system, there is likely to be a detrimental effect on this natural order.

There are now some 47,000 synthetic organic chemicals available for industrial use. Sooner or later they will all find their way into the ecosystem. No one knows what will happen.

"In other words, we have been blindly violating the rule that nature knows best. We have synthesized new, man-made organic chemicals because they are useful in transformers, or in killing insects, without first checking to see whether, being unnatural, they interfere with important life processes."[4]

(4) The Fourth Law of Ecology: *There Is No Such Thing as a Free Lunch*

"If everything is connected to everything else, and everything has to go somewhere, and if the cycles that are set up
by nature are best for it, the minute you barge in and try to
change the environmental system, it is going to cost you
something. . . . Now that we know how much it will cost to
clean up environmental pollution we realize that by polluting
the air, the soil, and the water, we have accumulated a huge
debt to nature."[5]

Barry Commoner admits to having borrowed this last law from
economics, yet the costs he is speaking of really have no place in the
classical equilibrium analysis. On the contrary, by admitting these
four laws into political economy, the classical harmony is effectively
destroyed—just as it is in the case of limited resources. Conversely,
the laws of ecology *are* economic laws. They refer directly and
explicitly to productive activities. If they are important to bionomics
and the condition of human existence on this planet, it would be folly
for political economy to ignore them.

Yet this is exactly what the economics profession does.[6] Questions
of bionomics are relegated to the category of "externalities"—external effects on firms—which "provide the standard exception to the
equation of optimality with universal perfect competition."[7] This is
a convenient ploy for the economists—in acknowledging that the
facts do not fit the theory they can, at the same time, relegate the
facts to the category of a substudy of exceptions to economic laws.
In this case, bionomics becomes a category of the theory of externalities. Externalities are an offshoot of welfare theory. Welfare theory
is a substudy of economic science.

Unfortunately this fragmented, reductionist approach to knowledge, which might be effectively applied to certain narrowly defined
technical and scientific problems, fails to yield a synthetic compre-
hension of the complex, interrelated system of capitalist political
economy. That is to say, as long as bionomic problems remain
dumped in the subsidiary class of "externalities," economic theory
as a whole will be external to, and incapable of dealing with, these
problems. The problems of "environmental spillover" do not "lend
themselves easily to analytic elegance."[8]

It is not the purpose of this chapter to provide an exhaustive
description of bionomic problems or to fully explore the ramifications these problems have upon political economy. Yet it would be
well to establish the magnitude of the task confronting the theorists.

The Club of Rome study concluded that virtually every measured pollutant is growing at an accelerating rate. Nearly all are growing faster than world population:

> Virtually every pollutant that has been measured as a function of time appears to be increasing exponentially. The rates of increase of the . . . [pollutants] . . . vary greatly, but most are growing faster than the population. Some pollutants are obviously directly related to population growth (or agricultural activity, which is related to population growth). Others are more closely related to the growth of industry and advances in technology.[9]

The most alarming statistic in the area of bionomics, however, comes as a result of a study Barry Commoner made of US agricultural and industrial production since World War II. He estimated that while United States production has about kept pace with population growth in the period from 1946 to 1971—increasing some 40 or 50 percent—the rise in pollution levels over the same twenty-five-year period was anywhere from 200 to 2,000 percent. In his own words:

> While production for the most basic needs—food, clothing, housing —has just about kept up with the 40 to 50 per cent or so increase in population (that is, production *per capita* has been essentially constant), the *kinds* of goods produced to meet these needs have changed drastically. New production technologies have displaced old ones. Soap powder has been displaced by synthetic detergents; natural fibers (cotton and wool) have been displaced by synthetic ones; steel and lumber have been displaced by aluminum, plastics, and concrete; railroad freight has been displaced by truck freight; returnable bottles have been displaced by nonreturnable ones. On the road, the low-powered automobile engines of the 1920's and 1930's have been displaced by high-powered ones. On the farm, while per capita production has remained about constant, the amount of harvested acreage has decreased; in effect, fertilizer has displaced land. Older methods of insect control have been displaced by synthetic insecticides, such as DDT, and for controlling weeds the cultivator has been displaced by the herbicide spray. Range-feeding of livestock has been displaced by feedlots. . . . This pattern of economic growth is the major reason for the environmental crisis. A good deal of the mystery and confusion about the sudden emergence of the environmental crisis can be removed by pinpointing, pollutant by pollutant, how the postwar technological transformation of the United States economy has produced not only the much-heralded 126 per cent rise in GNP, but also, at a rate about ten times faster than the growth of GNP, the rising levels of environmental pollution.[10]

A major problem standing in the way of corrective action is that pollution has no direct cost to the polluters. Marginal cost and marginal utility curves remain virtually unaffected, since the polluters are able to "externalize" these costs on other industries or consumers. For example, the suburban commuter drives a high-compression, four-thousand-pound automobile to work each day, yet does he, or General Motors for that matter, bear the cost of the damage inflicted by the car's exhaust on lungs, trees, clothing, and buildings? Do they bear the cost of oil spills from tankers carrying oil to be refined into gas for the car? The oil shippers and insurance companies certainly do not. They have lobbied hard to keep the responsibility off their shoulders.[11]

Or when municipalities and industries dump untreated wastes into Lake Erie, do they pay for the fishing industry and recreational facilities that are destroyed?

When Americans eat chickens containing dieldrin—a cancer-producing insecticide—does the grower or feed supplier or the supermarket pay a price for the illnesses which result?

When a power plant or a factory releases poisonous nitrogen oxides into the atmosphere, does that affect their equations of operating costs?

When Procter and Gamble replaced their soaps with detergents, were their profits hurt by the phosphate pollution that resulted?

The answer to these questions is obviously no. Since bionomic problems are alien to the classical theory of a market economy, why should political economy be concerned with them? Since they do not enter into the actual decision processes of profit-maximizing firms and pleasure-seeking individuals, should we simply forget the problem?

Bionomic concerns cannot be ignored, for two reasons. First, whether or not there is an immediate price attached to pollution or environmental destruction, the problems they cause are growing rapidly and having a profound effect on the ability of people to live a healthy life in decent surroundings, which, after all, is the asserted aim of all economic activity. Industrialists no longer point to belching smokestacks with pride—everyone now knows that air pollution has tarnished our standard of living. We can no longer eat natural foods without poisons and chemicals. Instead of the sounds of birds and the breeze, we hear the constant din of engines and machines. We see asphalt and automobiles where there were once trees and grass. Trash is everywhere; our cities are filthy. We see electric lights instead of the stars at night. Waters that were once clear and teeming with fish are now foul with chemicals and organic wastes. Increasingly, the statistics showing an evergrowing Gross National Product appear to be a cruel hoax.

The second reason for changing our outlook is that economic activities take place in the planet's ecosphere—the thin, life-sustaining environment of water, minerals, and organic activity. Ultimately, if we destroy our environment we destroy our economy, and ourselves. The plants, fish, and animals we eat come from that environment. The enormous quantities of energy and water consumed by industry, by transport, and in the home also come from nature. The value of conventional capital is ultimately dependent on biological capital. In an orgy of bionomic imperialism, capitalist civilization is now destroying our life-sustaining environment with an awesome ferocity.

In Commoner's view, a polluting industry is "borrowing" from the ecosystem's biological capital and creating a "debt to nature" for which the whole of society will ultimately have to pay. As conventional capital has accumulated, biological capital has declined:

> Since the usefulness of conventional capital in turn depends on the existence of the biological capital—the ecosystem—when the latter is destroyed, the usefulness of the former is also destroyed. Thus despite its apparent prosperity, in reality the system is being driven into bankruptcy. Environmental degradation represents a crucial, potentially fatal, *hidden* factor in the operation of the economic system.[12]

Commoner estimates that the costs of repaying in order to avert ecological catastrophe will be simply staggering. The cost for the United States alone would amount to some fifty billion dollars per year over the next twenty-five years (in current dollars). For an entire generation, much of the nation's capital resources would have to be devoted to rebuilding the environment, if the institutions of capital are to survive. New investments in agriculture, industry, and transport would have to be guided by bionomic considerations rather than conventional economic ones.[13] This means that sewage and garbage will have to be recycled. Wasteful packaging and no-return bottles will have to be eliminated. Agriculture will have to reduce the use of fertilizers and insecticides. The general dependence on automobile transportation will have to be severed. Natural fibers must replace synthetic ones. Land use will have to be governed by ecological considerations. Natural rubber must be used instead of synthetic, soap instead of detergents, and so on.

In short, technology must be reoriented to work within the natural laws—the human dependence upon nature must be recognized.

The competitive market operates on the basis of optimizing profit and pleasure. Since bionomic concerns don't enter into market equations, there is no way—repeat, no way—that these changes can be brought about through the outcome of the unencumbered market process. The "internalization" of bionomic concerns into the private decision-making processes would require a social magnanimity that would be contrary to the prevailing economic wisdom, from Adam Smith to Paul Samuelson. The triumph of the capitalist economic order was, in Marx and Engels's words, its "subjection of Nature's forces to man" to a degree unprecedented in all human history.[14]

It was characteristic of Marx that he should have noted a contradictory aspect to this triumph. He saw that the progress of capitalistic agriculture

> is a progress in the art, not only of robbing the laborer, but of robbing the soil; all progress in increasing the fertility of the soil for a given time, is a progress toward ruining the lasting sources of that fertility. The more a country starts its development on the foundation of modern industry, like the United States, for example, the more rapid is this process of destruction.[15]

It is an irony of history that in fighting capitalist exploitation, the workers have broadened the basis for capitalist prosperity which, as Adam Smith pointed out, is only as wide as the market. It is a double irony that nature, since it could not fight back, has been so thoroughly and brutally subjugated that it can no longer yield the same sustenance to industry. Capital has cut so much of nature's warp, and stretched it so far in the name of industry, that it is starting to rip.

When nature revolts, it is not turned back with inducements or arms. Solutions will have to be imaginative, complex, and costly. It is simple to destroy, complicated to rebuild. To expect that the same private initiative that is rending the global fabric can be called upon to reweave it, would be a supreme delusion. The tools of the market are not up to the task.

There is a close parallel and many interconnections between resource depletion and environmental degradation. Much the same can be said of their solution within a capitalist framework. But if anything, bionomic problems are more complex and unyielding. Theoretically, the resource problem could be attacked using input-output techniques—creating an overall use plan and setting specific industry allocations to which the market would be forced to adjust—although, as we pointed out, strict enforcement of such a plan would require such massive government intervention as to effectively rule out the market as an effective force in production decisions.

Bionomic problems are more intractable. Industry's ties with natural ecosystems are varied and complex. Just to lay bare the myriad of bionomic unknowns would require a massive, coordinated research effort. Meanwhile, the gulf between economic and ecological laws grows with every advance of technology.

Presuming the bionomic equations were filled in, the implementation of sound policies would again subject industry to a strong, centralized planning authority. Enormous capital expenditures would have to be carried out by the central authority itself—say, for rehabilitating rail and rapid transit—or mandated, as in the case of pollution controls. Already such inadequate controls as now exist are expected to cost industry many billions of dollars a year.

But that would only be a beginning. To fully implement sound bionomic policies the government would have to decide which industries could expand and where their plants could be located. It would have to establish strict standards over what chemicals could be used in agriculture and industry, and how much. Harmful products, such as aerosols, plastics, and the internal combustion engine, would be banned, regardless of how profitable they were. The authority would even decide which industrial processes are acceptable—whether solar power must be developed instead of nuclear; whether cattle can be fattened in feedlots or must stay down on the farm.

In short, there is no way that the environmental impact of economic activities can be internalized by profit-optimizing cost and utility functions. Bionomic studies are sure to show that bionomic laws negate economic ones, and vice versa.

When it comes to the environmental crisis, classical political economy is as dead as a dodo.

6

More Is Less

Society, in the utilitarian philosophy, is the algebraic sum of the individuals; and the interest of the society is the sum of the interests of the individuals.

Thorstein Veblen

At this point we need to take a look at the paradox of social poverty in a society endowed with unprecedented powers of production. How is it that the United States possesses one sixth of the world's wealth, yet our cities are decaying and a subway ride in New York is an ear-splitting, filthy, uncomfortable experience? How can more good bring less happiness? Is it because we have a class society? Is it due to corruption? Is it because we spend too much money on wars and not enough on public goods and services?

While those are factors, the principal reason lies deeper. It can be found in the presumed identity between the hedonistic calculus of the marketplace and the interests of society as a whole: the idea that an individual who buys or sells a commodity in the market is optimizing social good, as well as satisfying personal need. Such an identity may have been a fair approximation of the truth in Adam Smith's day, but in an era of mass consumption, urban living, and complex technologies, the proposition is no longer tenable.

Read the quote at the top of the page. Again. Thorstein Veblen had a knack for hacking pretentious argument away, leaving the philosophic pith exposed to our detached scrutiny. The above statement on the utilitarian philosophy is a case in point. We need only add to it the notions of supply and demand to arrive at the equilibrium theory which implies that whatever is, is good. And that, in essence, is the philosophy behind modern economic theory.

The way it works is simple. In a free market, people buy and sell as they please. If consumers want certain goods they will demand them. Businessmen will sense this demand through the marketplace and seek to satisfy the consumers' wishes. For example, if people want more shoes, they will bid up the market price. Manufacturers will find it profitable to step up their production to meet the increased demand. Prices will fall back and output will stabilize at the new level. Consumers have their shoes. Manufacturers still have their "normal" profits. Everyone is happy.

There is a lot to be said for this system. There is no need to set up a quota for shoes because if shoes are overproduced, they will not be sold at a reasonable profit. If shoes are underproduced, their extra profitability will cause a rise in output. The complex coordination of hundreds of individual decisions is done by the market. Profits provide the incentive to produce the right things or to stop producing the wrong things.

Yet the road from "society is the algebraic sum of the individuals" to "the interest of society is the sum of the interests of the individuals" is long and treacherous. Few economists seek to travel down it as Veblen did, for more than a little of the way. Most begin at the end. Individual demands and social good are simply equated, without showing why. Starting with Adam Smith's belief that government interference in trade usually did more harm than good, economic theory has gone through such an elaborate, rigorous refinement that it now confers the stamp of divine, ubiquitous intelligence to the humble transactions of the marketplace. In Veblen's words:

> By virtue of their hedonistic preconceptions, their habituation to the ways of pecuniary culture, and their unavowed animistic faith that nature is in the right, the classical economists knew that the consummation to which, in the nature of things, all things tend, is the frictionless and beneficent competitive system. This competitive ideal, therefore, affords the normal, and conformity to its requirements affords the test of absolute economic truth.[1]

Of course no economist believed that individuals themselves possess or exercise "absolute economic truth." Yet somehow the decisions of individuals, when lumped together, would. Given the distribution of income between rich and poor, social good was the product of individual demands. Individual demands had to be derived from utility. But utility in classical economics is a simple, psychological concept of pleasure or desire. The idea is useless as a basis of the theory of social value, since cumulative individualism has no social content. As Joan Robinson expressed it:

> *Utility* is a metaphysical concept of impregnable circularity; *utility* is the quality in commodities that makes individuals want to buy them, and the fact that individuals want to buy commodities shows that they have *utility*.[2]

When we bring economic reasoning to bear on the unfolding social economy, the concept of utility is an impediment to our understanding of the relationship between individual interest and social need.

This is not the place to explore how or why economics got itself into this predicament. But it must be pointed out that a relaxation of the belief in the optimality of the hedonistic decision process undermines the presumed efficacy of the competitive equilibrium. If the decisions and contracts freely entered into by individuals do not result in an approximate maximizing of the general welfare, the capitalist decision-making process can no longer have general validity.

According to theory, a society is making best use of its productive resources (provided there are no technological impediments) when prices are "at the level needed to bring forth the production necessary to supply the given level of demand."[3] That is, as long as markets are free of monopoly or other restrictions, prices will adjust themselves to the level where supply and demand are equated. People's needs will then be met to the fullest extent possible.

That is an adequate statement of the prevailing doctrine of how the social good is attained, but until the equation of individual demands to social need is put to the test—until the mechanisms are revealed by which anarchic, hedonistic economic motives are approximately translated into the ideal social allocation of resources—that supposedly scientific principle will be no more than a statement of faith that the operation of a competitive market tends toward some vague spiritual ideal.

Important as it is to recognize the spiritual character of that belief in the competitive ideal, it is more important to demonstrate why the free, competitive market is *not* the road to optimizing the interests of society. In applying the competitive ideal to the complex unfolding processes of capitalist institutions and technics, there are five vital points at which the market fails to deliver.

(1) To maximize self-gratification, perfect knowledge is necessary on the part of the consumer. But the belief that the consumer is able to make intelligent assessments of products was developed for a time when marketed goods were relatively simple and sensible. Judgments could be based upon experience and existing knowledge. How many people today can make intelligent selections of such complicated products as autos, refrigerators, toasters, synthetic textiles, powered lawnmowers, processed foods, and the like? Worse still, who can tell whether the tuna we eat contains mercury, or whether the vinyl chloride that was in Clairol hair spray will cause cancer of the liver?[4]

Two other factors make it difficult for consumers to judge products: advertising and obsolescence. Advertising which subtly appeals to subconscious human drives—as when Marlboro cigarettes are subliminally linked with vitality and sex appeal—impedes rather than aids our intelligence. Rapid obsolescence and product changes continually invalidate consumer knowledge. By the time experience has been gained on the new, a newer version is out. Consumer testing organizations have a hard time keeping up. Even if they could, the vast array of goods on the market overwhelms the individual consumer's capacity for rational choice, in the classical equilibrium sense.

Nor is perfect knowledge of the products from which one can choose any guarantee of happiness. Suppose our ideal consumer could size up every product in the market. Is he now in a position, dollar for dollar, to get the maximum fulfillment out of life?

Perhaps if we could have chosen not to invent the automobile, the telephone, the television, the jet plane, or the throwaway beer can, our lives would be happier today. "Primitive" cultures are quickly destroyed when exposed to modern inventions and institutions. Our complex materialistic culture may similarly place too much of a burden of knowledge on the individual . . . and too much faith in the products of General Motors and Standard Brands.

(2) Competitive theory assumes that goods demanded by consumers can be subdivided into small units. In the competitive market there are many buyers and many units of demand. "In reality, however, . . . 'it should be apparent at once that the theory of competitive equilibrium can cover only part of the economic field. An end

which cannot be atomised cannot be dealt with by an atomic analysis.' "[5] That is to say, many spending decisions cannot be made by autonomous individuals. Those decisions concern schooling, health programs, welfare, transportation, warfare, and most of the services required in an urban environment.

As the economy grows, the sphere of collective consumption grows faster than the sphere of private, atomistic consumption, which is theoretically subject to equilibrium analysis. Collective consumption now has a great impact on our lives. It would be difficult to overstress the importance of consumption decisions that are determined politically rather than through the competitive market. R. H. Tawney thought that the problem of collective spending was a major blind spot in the classical vision of the free market:

> In their enthusiasm at the spectacle of increasing profits and wages, which are the natural result of increased productivity, the philosophers of industrial civilization are disposed to interpret well-being as a commodity which, if unhampered by the State, individuals of character and intelligence can buy, in necessary quantities, like tea and sugar, by their own exertions.[6]

(3) To achieve a competitive optimum, we must also assume that one individual's consumption cannot affect another's pleasure. But what one person does with his money or property can have a major impact on the welfare of others. The wooded areas or farmlands that provide a community with fresh air, sensuous pleasures, and a feeling of freedom, may be bulldozed down by the owner to make way for suburban homes or a shopping center. The pleasure one gets from blasting a hi-fi may be a nuisance to one's neighbors. The person living next door to a pornographic book store, a McDonald's drive-in, or an airport is not likely to find consolation in knowing that those businesses supply pleasure and service for others. The automobile bought for business or pleasure also brings noise, dirt, poisonous fumes, congestion, visual blight, and danger to the community. The hundreds of pounds of waste generated per consumer creates monumental problems of disposal and pollution for the whole society. Background noise in most American cities exceeds the potentially damaging level of seventy decibels daily.[7] Nobody bought the noise for its own sake, yet it is the net result of autonomous decisions that are supposed to optimize our well-being. Hedonistic, equilibrium economics simply cannot cope with these growing "externalities" of private, individual demands and decisions.

(4) Production itself is seen to have no effect on an individual's well-being. Equilibrium analysis assumes that industrial technology is a neutral agent which has no effect on people's lives other than to deliver final products for consumption. Even if we ignore resource and environmental concerns, that postulate is wholly without foundation. Industry is very much a part of the surroundings in which people live and consume. To begin with, individuals spend much of their lives working and going to and from their places of employment. Aside from considering work a curse or sacrifice, economics looks only at how the lives of individuals are governed by consumption, to the neglect of that part of their experience which is shaped by their productive activities. Yet one's working life is a large portion of one's total experiences which shape one's self-perception and apprehension of the world at large. Its effect on one's physical and mental well-being is large and direct.

During their nonworking hours when workers are metamorphosed into consumers, the apparatus of industry and commerce do not disappear from the face of the earth. Factories, farms, stores, skyscrapers, wharves, mines, dams, railroads, trucks, and refineries assault our senses and affect our movement. They are as much a part of the consumer's condition as such consumption objects as food, clothing, homes, parks, cars, restaurants, and theaters. For its impact on people's lives, the industrial apparatus is as important a part of consumption as is private and collective consumption proper. One need only compare life in a rural, agrarian culture to that of an urban industrial one to discover that fact, yet economists are not cognizant of it. That indirect form of compulsory consumption falls well outside the pale of the hedonistic calculus of the marketplace.

(5) The element of time in equilibrium theory is completely arbitrary. Do we live for today? For the next ten years? How do we weigh the happiness of the next generation against our own? An economy cannot function without some time horizon. The time span of a market economy, which ranges from very short to a few years at most, may have worked well in the past, but today it is generally conceded to be too short. We are now paying a heavy price for many optimizing decisions made in the past. The vast growth in energy utilization, automobile transport, and the synthetic chemical industry since World War II now exerts an unforeseen burden on our daily lives. The market sees the immediate; the effects of its decisions have become increasingly long run and complex.

Certainly the manner in which cost functions are drawn up gives an accurate picture of how a firm generally operates. But the fact that a private business need not take the future costs of economic decisions into account for the purpose of its own profit maximization does not mean that we can ignore that time period when considering the needs of society. The factor of time creates a fundamental discrepancy between the accounting methods need for a firm or an individual and those needed for society. Therefore we can say that the more developed our economy becomes, the more complex it is, and the more economic processes affect the balance of nature and the availability of resources, the wider the gap will be between the results of short-term profit maximization and long-term (largely unmeasured) social needs. As capitalist production and technology evolve, short-term equations and long-term needs become more and more incompatible.

Those five theoretical failings are not the only reasons why the competitive market does not truly meet people's needs, but they should give us an idea of how limited the classical theory really is on this point. Let us conclude by noting that economic theory is attempting to utilize the laissez-faire mechanism, which was theoretically worked out for a rural farming and handicraft economy, by applying it to the vastly more complex, integrated, and urbanized industrial system. There is now every reason *not* to cling to the postulate that the interests of the individual and society are one; that the operation of a freely competitive market can possess some animistic quality by which self-serving decisions are imbued with a preternatural, teleological, benevolent intelligence.

7

The Pleasure Principle

Among all the several species of psychological entities, the names of which are to be found either in the *Table of the Springs of Action,* or in the *Explanations* subjoined to it, the two which are as it were the *roots,*—the main pillars or *foundations* of all the rest,—the *matter* of which all the rest are composed—or the *receptacles* of that matter,—which soever may be the *physical image,* employed to give *aid,* if not *existence* to conception,—will be, it is believed, if they have not been already, seen to be, PLEASURES and PAINS.

Jeremy Bentham

John Stuart Mill placed Jeremy Bentham, the English utilitarian philosopher, among the "masters of wisdom" whose writings "will long form an indispensable part of the education of the highest order of practical thinkers." Mill was critical of Bentham's conception of human nature, a conception limited by self-interest, but he still considered him to be the supreme illuminator of the business side of human affairs.

Marx was less impressed. To him Bentham was "the arch-Philistine . . . that insipid, pedantic, leather-tongued oracle of the ordinary bourgeois intelligence of the 19th century." He's not even a thinker in Marx's book, much less one of the "great intellectual benefactors of mankind."

Reading Bentham—and we seldom do these days—confirms Marx's sound judgment. It is hard to make any sense of Bentham. His murky reasoning and bumbling expressions are repugnant to our scientific, materialist outlook of the twentieth century. Could there ever have been a time when political economists hung on his every word? (And if Bentham was anything, he was a man of many words.)

Yet when we strip political economy, *any* political economy, of its outer trappings—when we look beneath the scientific reasoning and amoral objectivity—when we probe right down to the hard core of rationalism around which the argument is wound ... we find ... Bentham! Assume competition in any way or form, and it's hard to escape Jeremy Bentham's philosophy of pleasures and pains.

Because once the keystone of competition has been set into capitalist political economy, certain other principles fall into place. Among these are assumptions about human motives and social conduct. The flesh and blood of capitalism becomes the hedonistic "economic man" of classical political economy: those "lightning calculators of pleasures and pains," as Veblen called them, who interact in the marketplace, allocating resources or buying and selling commodities in an effort to obtain the means to achieve an optimum of self-gratification. The competitive model requires the assumption of a Benthamite logic which takes, in Marx's words, "the English shopkeeper as the normal man."

Economic man's only happiness is to increase his wealth and to live a life of ease and luxury. He is a perfect nihilist—his only ground for action is self-indulgence. It is no use to affirm, as Alfred Marshall and other bourgeois moralists were wont to do, that a belief in free enterprise still allows people to be motivated by love of God or country. Competitive political economy was built on the premise of a rational pursuit of personal gain.

The same can be said for more recent attempts to upgrade capitalist morality through the creation of the "soulful corporation" and other such guardians of the public interest. It might be all to the good if the nation's economic affairs could be governed by benevolent behemoths who, instead of trying to gain the upper hand in the competitive struggle for profits, sought to strike a judicious balance between the short- and long-term interests of stockholder, management, labor, consumers, and the public at large. But such behavior would wreak havoc with the economics of capitalism. By force of logic, it would mean that capital accumulation and competition have come to rest on charitable instincts. So far, no economist has had the temerity to assert the preeminence of such motives.

For in truth, economic hedonism lies at the foundation of the moral philosophy of the English Industrial Revolution and the pioneering capitalism of America. It is, in the words of R. H. Tawney:

The ... climax of generations of subtle moral change. The rise of modern economic relations, which may be dated in England from the latter half of the seventeenth century, was coincident with the growth of a political theory which replaced the conception of purpose by that of mechanism.[1]

The important idea here is that of "mechanism." Economic man is a fundamental element of economics, much like the elements of space, time, and matter are to physics. In his amoral quest for self-aggrandizement, economic man fortuitously and unwittingly serves the interests of the community at large. Even if his heartfelt desire were to serve society's interests first, an understanding of that purpose is beyond his grasp. He must rely on market feedback to tell him how to direct his investments or turn his labors to the most socially advantageous channels; he must chart his course with the pecuniary guidance of profits and wages. The market, not liberal sentiments, must serve as capitalism's guiding intelligence.

John Stuart Mill was sensitive to the attacks by the Romantic critics who saw in the materialism of the Enlightenment the debasement of the moral character and spiritual ideals of an earlier era. He realized, however, that that "arbitrary definition of a man" is an essential part of the competitive analysis. To the extent that people's behavior does not fit this mechanical conception, the classical analysis loses that much precision and force. Mill noted that the notion of custom was anathema to political economists, for the simple reason that it was incompatible with the operation of competitive principles.[2]

Yet to maintain this view puts economic theory in a strait jacket. However suitable this concept of human nature is for making abstract formulations of supply, demand, distribution, and exchange, it may not be an adequate basis from which to draw scientific inferences concerning actual investment behavior and the actions of workers and managers. An examination of economic man's fitness for fulfilling specific productive and investment functions may show a discrepancy between theory and reality.

Let us begin by taking a closer look at the logic of the concept. From the onset, it should be noted that, contrary to the mechanical nature of physical science, modern economic science operates on the basis of human reason and motive. While it is true that any science that has to do with human conduct must admit subjective cause, it is the peculiar weakness of hedonistic political economy that it is a narrowly based, closed, deductive system.[3] Such a scheme excludes many relevant cultural elements including received mores, political traditions, nonmaterial drives, and the changing roles of religion in relation to government and society.

Even in a fairly narrow context, there is much less sense to the concept of economic man than might appear. It is not clear that the motivational needs of a capitalistic economy would be fulfilled by the consistent, calculating, intelligent foresight of economic men behaving in accordance with Benthamite logic.

Consider the most important item of expenditure in a "capitalist" economy—capital investment. Would enough capital be forthcoming, on the basis of purely rational motives, to satisfy the economy's investment requirements? It is doubtful that it would, particularly since those who have the most to invest would, on the basis of the hedonist calculus, have the least to gain from a further accretion of their wealth. A rich individual would be less than rational to risk his capital in the hope of securing minor increases in comfort or security.

Since inequality is a touchy point, the concentration of wealth is not ordinarily a subject for study by government statisticians. The last direct survey of wealth holdings was conducted by the Census Bureau for the Federal Reserve Board in the spring and summer of 1963. The principal historical study we have was done by Robert J. Lampman in 1962 for the National Bureau of Economic Research. As the following table shows, the percentage of national wealth held by the top .5 percent of the adult population has remained relatively unchanged in recent years:[4]

1922	29.8
1929	32.4
1933	25.2
1939	28.0
1945	20.9
1949	19.3
1953	22.7
1954	22.5
1956	25.0
1962*	25.8
1969**	25.0

*Percent of total family wealth held by wealthiest .5 percent of all households. Dorothy S. Projector, "Survey of Financial Characteristics of Consumers," *Federal Reserve Bulletin*, March, 1964.

**Percent of net assets owned by the wealthiest .6 percent of the total population. Estimates by Lester C. Thurow based on Internal Revenue estate-tax data. Lester C. Thurow, *Generating Inequality* (New York: Basic Books, 1975), p. 15.

In 1969, the latest year for which estimates are available, the wealthiest .6 percent of the total population owned 25 percent of the

nation's wealth. To join that select group, an individual needed a minimum of $300,000 in net assets[5]—surely enough to ensure a modicum of comfort and security. Almost half of the wealth in this group was held by millionaires. And while those individuals at the top of the economic pyramid had 25 percent of the total wealth, they owned far more than one quarter of the private business capital. That is because much of the "wealth" of the middle classes consists of "consumer capital" such as homes and cars, or insurance and savings for old age or emergencies. The 1963 census showed that for families with net worth in the $25,000–$50,000 range, two thirds of their assets were in homes, cars, liquid assets, and life insurance. For families in the $500,000-and-over class, only 10 percent of their assets were tied up in those nonbusiness, nor investment categories.[6]

The Lampman study showed that the top 1 percent of the adult population that owned 24 percent of the private wealth in the United States in 1953 actually owned approximately 76 percent of all corporate stock, 100 percent of state and local bonds, 32 percent of federal bonds, and 78 percent of other bonds.[7] Much of that vast wealth was in the hands of individuals who had the least to gain in terms of rational, hedonistic calculus, and little incentive for risk-taking.

John Maynard Keynes, an astute speculator himself, had this to say about the investment propensities of economic man. In *The General Theory* he wrote:

> If human nature felt no temptation to take a chance, no satisfaction (profit apart) in constructing a factory, a railway, a mine or a farm, there might not be much investment merely as a result of cold calculation. . . . Most, probably, of our decisions to do something positive, the full consequences of which will be drawn out over many days to come, can only be taken as a result of animal spirits—of a spontaneous urge to action rather than inaction, and not as the outcome of a weighted average of quantitative benefits multiplied by quantitative probabilities. . . . Thus if the animal spirits are dimmed and the spontaneous optimism falters, leaving us to depend on nothing but a mathematical expectation, enterprise will fade and die;—though fears of loss may have a basis no more reasonable than hopes of profit had before.[8]

In other words, the capitalists, or potential capitalists, in a competitive society, must be possessed by an accumulative drive which is external to the conception of the rational calculus. Without this modification of an otherwise simple, homogeneous approach to human behavior, there will be few to risk the perils of competitive capitalist struggle. Once a capitalist economy has evolved to a high level of accumulation, and wealth is concentrated in the hands of a small segment of the population, it is ludicrous to attribute the continued competitive and accumulative drive, which often goes under the insipid term of "entrepreneurship," to a predilection for deferred gratification. If a capitalist can retire comfortably today, why should he strive to aggrandize his wealth further, even if the risk appears small? Were wealth desired only as a means to increased security and consumer-satisfactions, accumulation would grind to a halt.

The top dogs in a capitalist order, therefore, cannot possibly be purely economic beings. Gaining, not gain, according to Marx, must be their principal aim.[9] Or as Veblen put it:

So far as regards those members and classes of the community who are chiefly concerned in the accumulation of wealth, the incentive of subsistence or of physical comfort never plays a considerable part. Ownership began and grew into a human institution on grounds unrelated to the subsistence minimum. The dominant incentive was from the onset the invidious distinction attached to wealth, and, save temporarily and by exception, no other motive has usurped the primacy at any later stage of the development.[10]

That presents us with a paradox. On the one hand, abstract theory shows us that competitive capitalism functions on the basis of rational, calculating, purely economic motives—ultimately upon the desire of each individual in society for optimum material self-gratification. The "invisible hand" of the competitive market mechanism harmonizes potentially conflicting individual drives and provides them with the tangible satisfactions they are striving for. On the other hand, competitive capitalism cannot possibly function without attributing motives that are irrational, from an economic standpoint, to those individuals in whose power and upon whose decisions the survival of capitalism depends.

Part of the answer to this paradox might lie in the increasing institutionalization of economic decisions. It may be, for example, that corporations and financial trustees serve as surrogate individuals with insatiable desires. Monopoly, with its economic power and political control—its ability, as Galbraith put it, to establish planned, stable prices and markets—may encourage investment by reducing uncertainties.[11] And most important, government, through fiscal and monetary control, regulation of markets, subsidization of research and development, and other policies aimed at increasing business security and encouraging growth, may underwrite the economy by playing the role of the *irrational* investor and by taking risks no sane, economic man would assume.

Let us move on now from the problem of investment to that of production. After Smith's time, economics became essentially a science of distribution. In Ricardo's day, particularly at the time of the Corn Law controversies in the early 1800s, the principal problem of political economy became the manner in which the income of the nation was shared among landlords, capitalists, and workers.[12] Aside from the laws of diminishing returns and comparative advantage, little consideration was given to questions of actual production. Modern theories especially are "construed in terms of ownership, price and acquisition; and so reduce themselves in substance to doctrines of distributive acquisition."[13] In such a plan, production is largely a consequence of consumer demand.

As economics became increasingly preoccupied with the mathematical equation of supply and demand, it was rare to find economists who had more than a superficial idea of the relation between economic motive and industrial progress. Veblen was a major exception. He drew a sharp contrast between the traits which promote industrial efficiency and the motives characteristic of competitive business:

> The collective interests of any modern community center in industrial efficiency. The individual is serviceable for the ends of the community somewhat in proportion to his efficiency in the productive employments vulgarly so called. This collective interest is best served by honesty, diligence, peacefulness, good-will, an absence of self-seeking, and an habitual recognition and apprehension of causal sequence. . . .

> On the other hand, the immediate interest of the individual under the competitive regime is best served by shrewd trading and unscrupulous management. The characteristics named above as serving the interests of the community are disserviceable to the individual. . . . Under the regime of emulation the members of a modern industrial community are rivals, each of whom will best attain his individual and immediate advantage if, through an exceptional exemption from scruple, he is able serenely to overreach and injure his fellows when the chance offers.[14]

In other words, the smooth functioning of a modern economy requires economic sense to be tempered by fair dealing and integrity.

Producers should be motivated by a dedication to a higher purpose —a commitment not likely to be fostered by an anarchic, competitive régime. If our economic man is not a reliable investor, neither is he, according to Veblen, a trustworthy producer.

Veblen's main concern was to show how the behavior of modern businessmen was becoming increasingly at odds with industrial (i.e., public) purpose. But are the motives of the workers under modern capitalism any more suited to promoting the larger good than those of the businessmen?

During the early days of the Industrial Revolution, the motives of the working class did not resemble those of the abstract economic man. During that era, particularly in England, land became monopolized, yeomenry was suppressed, craft organizations were destroyed, and men, women, and children were literally being turned into "wage slaves." Mumford wrote that they were being

> Reduced to the function of a cog, the new worker could not operate without being joined to a machine. Since the workers lacked the capitalists' incentives of gain and social opportunity, the only things that kept them bound to the machine were starvation, ignorance, and fear. These three conditions were the foundations of industrial discipline, and they were retained by the directing classes even though the poverty of the worker undermined and periodically ruined the sytem of mass production which the new factory discipline promoted.[15]

As Marx pointed out, the Benthamite psychology applied (roughly) only to the bourgeois strata. The motivation for the mass of mankind was not the shopkeeper's rational calculation, but an enforced subservience at the hands of capital.

This enforced discipline, coupled with the vestiges of the earlier agrarian and craft traditions, created a vast store of exploitable human resources as industry emerged from the feudal era. Inevitably, mass consumption and mass education were to undermine the new machine discipline. Workers acquired their own personal ambitions. No longer faced with starvation, they emigrated to new opportunities or organized for shorter hours and better pay. "Education and experience have destroyed the passivity which was the condition of the perpetuation of industrial government in the hands of an oligarchy of private capitalists."[16]

Actually, at the time competitive political economy originated, the line between capital and labor was not always sharply drawn. The doctrine of freedom of enterprise, that each individual had the right to secure his property and to utilize it as he saw fit, was originally bound up with the image of the small entrepreneur—the independent proprietor or master craftsman. His capital did not consist of a mass of industrial machinery and stores of raw material. No stocks or bonds were floated for the purpose of centralizing capital into corporate organizations employing hundreds of workers. Even in his celebrated example of the pin factory, Smith portrays an organization of ten or twenty workmen brought together under one roof. In fact, when Smith rails against conspiracies to restrain trade and raise prices, when he decries the effects that corporations have in weakening competitive discipline, he is often speaking of the intrigues and organizations not of capitalists, but of the independent classes of artificers and manufacturers.[17]

In the eyes of the proponents of natural rights, capital had not acquired the power of subjugating man to man.[18] On the contrary, its free exercise was considered to be an essential condition for liberty. In England, the idea of right served as a barrier to government encroachment. When revolution came to France in 1789, it was

> ... in the name of rights of property [that] France abolished in three years a great mass of property rights which, under the old régime had robbed the peasant of part of the produce of his labor....[19]

In short, concepts of "natural rights" and "economic man" which were the spiritual foundation of capitalism were, in the beginning, inseparable from the notion of proprietorship. This conception of the rights of man assumed a primitive unity between labor and capital. The actual establishment of full-blown capitalist relations involved more than just the progress of invention and the amassing of machinery; it meant the extinction of the independent classes of craftsmen and peasant proprietors. Modern economic man is an investor or consumer, rarely an independent producer. The worker, it is assumed, will still seek out the most advantageous occupation; but only as a consumer does he play any role in determining what is produced. As an economic man, he is a pale image of his former self.

How can producers who are no longer proprietors be motivated? Considered abstractly, it would still appear that, despite the divorce between capital and labor, there is every incentive for a worker to do a good job. It is in his interest to win favor with his employer, to advance his position and receive a high wage. Even if the connection between service and reward is a tenuous one, to whatever extent one exists, it should be in the worker's interest to seek the maximum gain. The pursuit of self-interest should also lead a worker to search out and to secure the education and skills to enhance his industrial efficacy, and the type of employment best suited to his abilities.

While the existence of such worker motivation appears self-evident, it is not easily reconciled with another fundamental proposition of classical political economy—the aversion to labor. Stated simply, in terms of that fundamental Benthamite psychology of pleasures and pains . . . work is a pain.

Of course, the pain incurred through productive labors cannot be construed to be an effect unique to capitalist social relations. Yet there are several reasons why this admittedly archaic psychological dichotomy is particularly apt in its description of what motivates the laborer under capitalism.

Under capitalism the worker is prevented from owning the tools and other means of production that would enable him to earn an independent livelihood. He is forced to sell his labor power to the capitalist. Instead of employing capital to do his work, the capital employs him. Since the return on his labor, over and above what he receives in wages, accrues to the capitalist, the worker has only an incidental interest in the efficiency of his labors or the profitability of its employment. Shall we say, still employing our crude psychology, that there is no direct connection between his pleasures and his pains? Adam Smith astutely perceived that:

> A poor independent workman will generally be more industrious than even a journeyman who works by the piece. The one enjoys the whole produce of his own industry; the other shares it with his master.[20]

Modern industry and trade are based upon a multitude of complex and varied processes and are carried out through an intricate process of communication and cooperation. It is evident from the start that the modern work-process requires a great deal of surveillance, coordination, and control. Under capitalism, that is primarily developed not by the workers themselves but by those who represent the interests of capital.[21]

But the passive acceptance by the worker of externally imposed supervision further inhibits an active interest in doing a good job. The imposed discipline only undermines the worker's self-discipline and professional pride:

> If confidence is necessary to the investment of capital, confidence is not less necessary to the effective performance of labor by men whose

sole livelihood depends upon it. If they are not yet strong enough to impose their will, they are strong enough to resist when their masters would impose theirs. They may work rather than strike. But they will work to escape dismissal, not for the greater glory of a system in which they do not believe.[22]

When workers impose a slowdown in industry by working "by the rules," it should be evident that a great deal of creative cooperation is normally required to get the job done. Yet very few people can be found today who believe in, and work for, "the greater glory of a system." Most workers follow the path of least resistance. The pecuniary motive, plus a moderate amount of fear and pride, encourages them to fulfill established routines and perform a moderate amount of work. Few take an active interest in the success of the enterprise or feel impelled to improve the efficiency or effectiveness of their tasks.

The worker with creative intelligence is a threat. For the purpose of control, managers often make work as repetitive and degrading as possible. This may impair the efficiency of labor for any but the meanest tasks, but much success has been achieved in "Tayloring" many jobs to fit the conception of the worker as a semiliterate robot.[23] Now, of course, employers moan that "you can't get good workers any more" . . . which only affirms their patronizing policies.

The true costs of social anarchy, of a system of production not directed toward a higher goal than private gain, result from the feeling of disinterest, detachment, and apathy on the part of the worker. The worker can be prodded by the fear of the loss of job or income, but very little can be done to encourage him to creatively participate in the collective labors of the enterprise. Divorced from ownership and its rewards, totally removed from the joint management of the corporation, ignorant even of the role he plays in its success, there is no way that the worker can be induced to share the goals of management. He is assigned a role that is no part of his making and generally opposed to his own interests. To the extent that these goals are effectively forced upon him, management will engender the worker's ill will.

In his hostility toward management, the worker is only reciprocating management's feelings toward him. Many managers look upon the worker merely with an eye to their industrial serviceability. Often employers will think nothing of risking injury or death to the worker if the costs of prevention outweigh the probable pecuniary penalty.[24] Nor if the worker's industrial serviceability is impaired by age, ill health, or the shifting fortunes of industry will those in whose hands the corporation's vitality is entrusted hesitate to unceremoniously propel such unwanted human material onto the rubbish heap of retirement or into the industrial reserve army.

The antagonism between capital and labor is in no way diminished by the intervention of unions to protect the rights of the workers. Any mitigation of the worker's circumstances won through collective struggle is not perceived as an indication of industrial harmony or the beginnings of a new era of corporate benevolence. Paternalistic management never extends to giving the worker a vested stake in the business through a substantial sharing of profits and responsibilities, although it may try hard to present such appearances.

On the other hand, it is quite in keeping with the precepts of the hedonistic calculus for workers to more or less systematically obstruct productive processes. Less efficient ways generally mean more employment and overtime. And no matter what the process, it is to the worker's benefit to see that the job is done as slowly as possible. This is quite a contrast to the classical pin factory in which the laborer had a direct, or at least an indirect, proprietary interest in his work.

When the separation of ownership from control assumes the most advanced, corporate forms, that indifference to the success of the enterprise tends to drift upward, to infect the middle and upper reaches of the organization. In a large-scale bureaucracy, no local manager is expected to form an objective assessment of the importance of his unit. It is commonly assumed that he will seek to further his personal aggrandizement by overstressing his unit's importance and overestimating the expenses needed to carry out its functions. Furthermore, he will seek to overfulfill his goals by keeping the demands placed upon it to a minimum. A frank admission that the corporate interests would be best served by the paring of one's unit's functions or scope is abnormal, a risky political ploy at best. At a recent budget hearing, members of the New York City Council were astounded when one official voluntarily struck some unneeded funds from his agency's budget.

Within the corporate or governmental bureaucracy itself, there is a constant urge, on the part of decision makers, to siphon off a portion of the collective funds for their private use. The devices through which this is accomplished are as ingenious as they are numerous. They run the gamut from corporate cars, vacations, and personal expenses to kickbacks to dummy subcontractors and the most subtle and elaborate conflicts of interest. The very term "conflict of interest" denotes a more or less systematic deviation of the interests of the hedonistic official from that of the corporate or governmental collective.

Ralph Nader's Corporate Accountability Research Group calculated that in 1974, the average annual upkeep for chief executives among the nation's top corporations—salary, bonus, stock options, apartments, chauffeured limousines and other creature comforts—came to $600,000 to $700,000.[25] In the ordinary run of business, there is continuous guerrilla warfare between individual and corporate interests. Bureaucrats often engage in tactical maneuvers to use their corporate positions for personal gain.

One recent case that dealt with this problem involved a suit against Penphil, an "insiders" investment club formed by some high-ranking Penn Central officers and outside associates before the Penn Central's collapse. A suit brought by the railroad alleged that these officers used the railroad's resources for Penphil's and their own profit.[26]

Thus a primary result of the evolution of modern enterprise, for both workers and managers, has been the separation of industry from its rewards. In place of the mechanism of self-interest, modern business has had to install an elaborate system of industrial standardization, surveillance, and control. An army of engineers, efficiency experts, accountants, and managers has been created, in large part to perform the role of surrogate proprietors, both to oversee the workers and to ensure that the managers themselves put corporate interests before their own. Obviously, this modern process of industrial standardization and control had the overall goal of raising productivity and profits. It succeeded mightily, in many instances, in achieving this end. But we must not overlook the fact that the surveillance and direction of an advanced capitalist economy is a far more complex, costly and bureaucratic affair than it would otherwise be if the self-interest of workers and managers coincided with the interests of productive enterprise.

As time goes on, the cultural and economic organization of that society based upon the profit motive witnesses a steady decline in the efficacy of its principles. Of course, no society could ever function upon hedonistic motives alone. Government has always been called upon to secure public monies and the power of the state to provide the services or force, if necessary, to guarantee the success of private ventures. But capitalism's strength has been its appeal to, indeed its dependence upon, rational self-interest.

Unfortunately it is equally in capital's self-interest to distort or destroy the competitive framework. It is eminently sensible for a banker to withdraw money from urban housing and business to squander it in constructing a nuclear power plant. His former investment was tied up with common people or at best small businessmen in a decaying competitive market. In the latter case, he deals comfortably with fellow bureaucrats in his world of loopholes and guarantees.

To Mumford, the ascendancy of pecuniary values that took place at the time of the Industrial Revolution meant more than the transformation of our mode of thinking, our means of production, our manner of living: it was a sign that the fabric of social order was coming apart.[27] Perhaps today, as our economy and society appear to be "ascending into barbarism," as economic and social forces appear increasingly irrational and destructive, it is time we questioned the serviceability of the Benthamite psychology. In retrospect, the success of capital, with its self-seeking motives, may have been peculiar to the era when there were new worlds to conquer—to the historic circumstance in which the growth of industrial efficiency outstripped the pace of corporate consolidation and the drift toward ecological, social, and political disaster.

8

The Corporate Domain

The management of power in a complex society is built around institutions. In our country, the most enduring, coordinated and generic manager of power is the corporate institution. Controlling great wealth and metabolized by the most fungible of factors —the dollar—the modern corporation possesses a formidable unity of motivation and action with great stamina.

Ralph Nader

Competition is an elusive concept. On the one hand, it is a dynamic force—the driving impulse to the engine of capital accumulation. On the other, the notion of competition has been abstracted and refined by neoclassical economists into a pure, mathematical essence —they have taken a powerful idea and transformed it into an elaborate status quo ideology.

There is nothing technically wrong with the mathematical concepts. There is nothing that cannot be explained within the neoclassical framework, given enough refinements, exceptions, and "exogenous factors." For that matter, we can still describe celestial motions as if the earth were the center of the universe. But what we are left with is a purely formal system that gives no sense of organic unity or progress. It is all-encompassing, yet woefully complex and incomprehensible. The neoclassical theories might explain what took place in the past without giving us the slightest hint of what to expect in the future. As Veblen said of Alfred Marshall, the leading British economist at the turn of the century:

Any sympathetic reader of Professor Marshall's great work . . . comes away with a sense of swift and smooth movement and interaction of parts; but it is the movement of a consummately conceived and self-balanced mechanism, not that of a cumulatively unfolding process or an institutional adaptation to cumulatively unfolding exigencies.[1]

Those words are especially true of neoclassical economics today. The continued, singular dependence upon the competitive, or modified competitive, model as the source of all economic wisdom (whether by design or default) has bred academic elegance at the cost of relevance. The "pure" competition of the textbooks is nothing more than a state in which all individuals have optimized their pleasure and no one has the power to attain more than their share of "utils."

In fact, such refined competition is really not competition at all. Prices are stable. Supply and demand are equated. No individual buyer or seller exerts any control over the market. There is perfect knowledge, no uncertainty, and the rate of profit is everywhere the same. The level of output remains constant, or at least whatever growth occurs should be steady and risk-free. Strictly applied in its usual static context, the logic of neoclassical competition negates capitalism itself.

The main lesson to be learned from this is that the importance of competition can only be seen in a dynamic context. The early classical economists had a conception of competition at once both cruder and more sophisticated than that of their twentieth century successors. They saw competition as a vital process—real struggles and conflicts in an ever-changing, uncertain world. They thought of competition as a cumulative unfolding of events rather than a stalemate of opposing forces. If political economy is to be relevant again, it must dispense with some of its elegant mathematical refinements and return to that rough-and-ready theory of competition which deals with the myriad of forces in the real world.

What happens if we treat competition as a force in an unfolding, historical process instead of as a means to fixing a balance between opposing forces? The end product is no longer the static equilibrium of pure competition; it is industrial consolidation. In the end, monopoly. After all, what is competition among entrepreneurs if it is not a means for rewarding the efficient and weeding out the weak from the strong?[2] "A casting out of business men by the chief of business men."[3] This logical outgrowth of industrial concentration is one that economists have sought to ignore by divorcing competition from the process of accumulation.

This trend toward big business is a discordant intrusion upon the theme of market harmony. Originally the classical concept of entre-preneurship had to be liberally stretched to cover the emergent joint stock company, or corporation. These companies embodied collec-tive ownership within the protective legal form of limited responsibil-ity and accountability. Then toward the close of the nineteenth century the modern system of credit capital came to full maturity, with the formation of powerful banking interests and a number of industrial trusts. This was asking too much of the old order. Louis D. Brandeis and other critics rightly regarded these consolidated forms of ownership and finance as a peril to both economic function and political democracy.

Today we are in an age in which most significant industries are giving way to monopoly control. The gross auto product alone amounts to some $60 billion, produced mostly by a handful of firms. The nine largest oil companies earned $7 billion in 1973.[4] It is taken for granted that most of the telephones in the nation are controlled by a single "public utility" (i.e., private monopoly) and that in each state only one or two firms supply all of the electricity or natural gas.[5] There are only half a dozen or so major airlines. Most television stations are controlled by three networks. In Washington, D.C., the bulk of all food is supplied by three supermarket chains. Huge finan-cial empires predominate in banking and insurance. Two companies make up most of the photographic industry. Single firms dominate the computer and office copier fields. We could go on and on to show that bigness is becoming the rule and that individual, freely competi-tive enterprise is being relegated to the backwaters of the economy.

A measure of the monopolistic control over individual markets is shown by the concentration ratios in manufacturing industries. These are compiled every five years by the U.S. Census Bureau.[6] The term "concentration ratio" is applied to the percentage share of the total activity (measured usually by the value of shipments) of a particular segment of industry accounted for by the largest compa-nies in that sector.

The statistics for 1972, the most recent available, show that out of one hundred thirty-five producers of elevators and escalators, the four largest account for 55 percent of the shipments. For the eight largest companies the figure was 68 percent and the twenty largest producers together supplied 82 percent of the product. What these figures indicate is that the largest producers of elevators and escala-tors probably have the potential to exercise considerable control over output and prices.

The graph which follows provides a rough measure of the degree of industrial concentration for the year 1972. Each industry is grouped into one of three concentration-level classes.[7]

Individual industries are too small to show up on the graph. Instead, what is shown are the Major Groups to which they are assigned in the Standard Industrial Classification (SIC) system. Thus most industries in the transportation group were at the high end of the concentration scale. Industries in the food group were scattered, though they leaned a bit towards the low end of the scale.

Looking at the industrial economy as a whole, 30 percent of total output was produced by industries with four company concentration ratios in excess of 50 percent. Another 38 percent had ratios in the 25–49 percent range, while only 32 percent of the shipments came from industries in which the concentration was less than 25 percent. On the basis of those statistics, it seems safe to say that the industries in which competitive conditions approach that of the classical model are the exception, not the rule, under modern conditions.

Another source of concentration data is *Fortune*'s annual lists of the largest corporations in the United States. Of the hundreds of thousands of industrial corporations, the five hundred to make *Fortune*'s industrial list had sales of $971 billion in 1976 employed 14,836,163 workers and garnered $49 billion in profits. Even the last company on the list, Foxboro, had $328 million in sales and 9,761 employees.[8] In 1974, the last year for which comparisons could be made, the top 500 accounted for two thirds of the sales and seven tenths of the profits of all industrial companies.

Fortune's "fifty largest" lists of commercial banking companies, life-insurance firms, diversified financial enterprises, retailers, transportation companies, and utilities show that big business predominates beyond the industrial field.

The fifty biggest banks had assets of $582 billion. The fifty life-insurance companies had assets of $257 billion; the top diversified financial companies, $172 billion. The fifty biggest retailers had sales of $133 billion and employed 2,744,513 workers. *Fortune*'s transportation companies had revenues of $42 billion. The monopoly power of the fifty biggest utilities is reflected by their assets of $253 billion and their $95 billion in revenues.

Economists used to be fond of pointing to the agricultural sector of the economy as the best example of free competition. Now in the days of international grain deals, feed lots, chicken factories, giant canners, and food processors, "agribusiness" has become a way of

Manufacturing Industries by Concentration Class 1972

Value of Shipments in Billions of Dollars

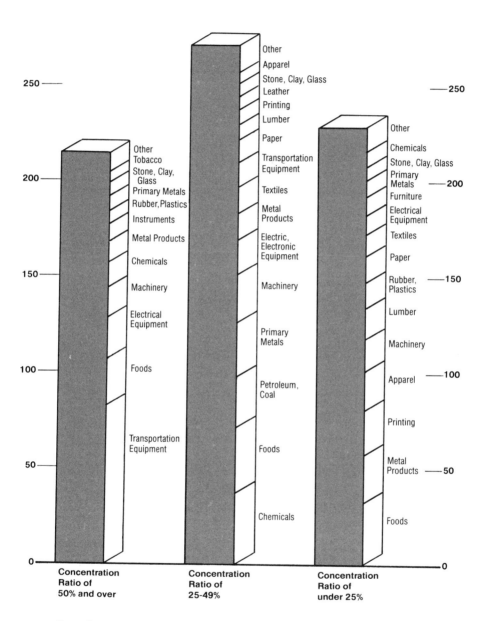

Source: *Concentration Ratios in Manufacturing*, U.S. Department of Commerce, Bureau of the Census,
U.S. Government Printing Office, Washington, D.C., 1975.

life. During the decade of the 1960s, large farms increased their share of the total farm income from 18 percent to 43 percent.[9] While farmers are still quitting the land at a rate of 100,000 a year, new corporate entries are moving into the "food supply systems" business. They go by such unlikely names as Tenneco, Kaiser Aluminum, Southern Pacific, and Dow Chemical.[10] The small farmers that are left eke out a marginal existence, squeezed between suppliers, bankers, transportation and storage companies, canneries, and food processors.

A second layer of monopoly control lies, mostly hidden, underneath the first. An important development in that respect of late has been the rapid growth of institutional investment portfolios, particularly commercial bank holdings. Although the banks are not usually permitted to own common stocks on their own account, their trust departments supervise large holdings for pension funds, estates, and other trust and custody accounts. In 1969 the fifty largest bank trust departments administered $131 billion in common stocks, exercising sole voting authority for an estimated $72 billion out of that total.[11] The massive centralization of nominal authority puts those banks "in a position where they can exert significant influence, through voting and otherwise, on corporate decisions and policies."[12]

For example, the competing airlines, UAL and American Airlines, have something in common normally invisible to the public eye. They each have more than 20 percent of their common stock held in accounts of the big New York banks.[13] It would hardly require an inordinate amount of circumspection among all parties concerned—the actual stockholders, the trustees, and the airlines themselves —to see that cutthroat competition would be inadvisable.

Broadcasting is another example. Who would suspect that the Chase Manhattan Bank has sole or partial voting rights to 14 percent of the stock in the Columbia Broadcasting System? (A holding of 5–10 percent of the stock is generally enough to control a corporation.[14]) It is doubtful that they have broadcast in the evening news that one of the bank's directors sits on the board of CBS.[15]

Banks and other financial institutions also serve as convenient mechanisms for circumventing antitrust laws. The Clayton Act forbids directors of competing oil companies to sit on each other's boards. But this does not stop sixteen directors of seven different oil companies from sitting together on Citibank's board.[16] These indirect interlocks are within the letter of the law.

Business has come a long way from the independent entrepreneur of Adam Smith's era who employed a handful of workers. Giant centers of corporate control are the predominant feature of modern capitalism. All this agglomeration of wealth and power is the end product of the evolutionary forces at work in the competitive process.

With the powers of production, marketing, finance, and even buying so highly centralized, how are the traditional decision-making processes of political economy affected? How is the functioning of markets influenced by the new institutional arrangement?

In conventional analysis, monopoly is a perversion of the normal state of perfect competition, not an institution in its own right. Most economists wish to believe that the principal theoretical difference between the behavior of a competitive firm and that of a monopolistic one is that the former faces a horizontal "revenue curve," the latter a downward-sloping one:

> Equilibrium for the firm under perfect competition can only occur when the marginal cost curve of the firm is rising at and near equilibrium output. Equilibrium under monopoly can occur whether marginal costs are rising, falling or constant.[17]

In plain language, if a firm can restrict the entry of rivals into an industry, then it is likely to earn supernormal profits over an extended period of time. Its market behavior becomes circumspect. It can consider the effects of its production and pricing decisions on total market demand and the decisions of rival firms. The attempt will usually be made, individually and in concert with other firms, to increase profits by restricting output and increasing prices.[18]

Thus the prevailing theory supports Gardiner Means's conclusion that monopolistic, administered competition results in higher prices and lower output than under the competitive norm. In his book *The Structure of the American Economy,*[19] he analyzed the 1935 concentration data and found that it pointed to a significant degree of concentration in the manufacturing field as a whole. In contemporaneous studies of price movements, he also found that many prices are not determined by the traditional equation of supply and demand, that there was an "administered market in which production and demand are equated at an inflexible administered price."[20] Particularly in concentrated industries, prices are frequently unresponsive to changes in demand. When demand falls in an administered market, firms are more likely to cut back their output than to reduce their prices, as they are supposed to do under pure competition.

On the other hand, it is less clear how overall distribution would be affected by monopolistic pricing. For one thing, it has not been demonstrated that a prevalence of monopolized markets would result in a reduction of labor's share of the total product. Big business must still compete for labor in the market and it is a target for unionization. If labor does maintain its share of the total product under monoply, it follows that the tolls taken by each monopoly would tend to cancel each other out. The more strategically placed monopolies would profit most, but their "excess" gains would be net of the gains extracted by less well placed monopolies. If that is the case, the distribution of income may not be so affected as would first appear, though there may be less income to distribute.

There are several other issues of monopoly theory of varying theoretical importance. They are:

(1) Innovation is slowed under monopoly.[21]

(2) There is a growth of wasteful, nonprice types of competitive selling, such as advertising and product differentiation.[22]

(3) Owing to varied elasticities of demand and other technical factors, the allocation of resources and commodity outputs are altered (and total utility diminished) from what they would be under a meticulously balanced competitive régime.[23]

What appears to be a more critical problem of monopoly capitalism is the inflationary bias caused by the downward rigidity of administered prices.[24] In times of business slump, the resulting cutbacks in production, rather than prices, might hamper the normal self-correcting mechanisms of the economy. The latter problem seems to have been, at least implicitly, a principle focus of Keynes's analysis. Say's Law (that production creates its own demand), which Keynes rejected, was a legitimate expression of the doctrine of competitive equilibrium. Monopolistic rigidities and imperfections leave a gap in private demand. Keynes postulated that it was government's job to fill the gap. Unfortunately, other than in the most severe periods of business depression, efforts to balance monopoly demand and supply further unbalance credit and prices. Keynes never solved this problem of "administered inflation." Presumably government policies to maintain high employment would always leave a residue of rising prices.

Today the American economy does not resemble the competitive model in which firms are small, mobile, and without influence over the market for their products. It would be more accurate to say that business is a system of power—to a large extent the corporation seeks to control the exigencies of the marketplace and escape the buffeting winds of competition. The competition that remains tends to degenerate into an increasingly tactical struggle, involving not only administered pricing, collusive bidding, advertising, and the fixing of market shares, but also the struggle between industrialists to control the strategic interstices of the economy.[25]

Today there is every evidence that corporate consolidation represents not industrial efficiency so much as strategic power—marketing, financial and political power. The giant, integrated industrial works, of which Henry Ford's River Rouge colossus was a famous example, have been outmoded by the new decentralized technologies in energy, transport, materials, machine design, and electronics.[26] Though there are now only four U.S. auto makers, their domestic car manufacturing operations are dispersed among 317 separate plants in 32 different states.[27] Clearly, it is more than technological necessity that keeps the auto giants in control.

The auto industry has used its consolidated power to win some major economic battles. A notable success was General Motors' campaign to scrap local trolley systems in favor of GM buses. In 1932 GM formed the United Cities Motor Transit as a subsidiary of its bus division. The sole function of this holding company "was to acquire electric streetcar companies, convert them to GM motorbus operation, and then resell the properties to local concerns which agreed to purchase GM bus replacements."[28]

Its first victims were the electric streetcar lines of Kalamazoo and Saginaw, Michigan, and Springfield, Ohio. In 1936 GM combined with the Omnibus Corporation to convert the New York trolley system, at the time the world's largest, in the short span of eighteen months. General Motors then joined forces with Standard Oil of California, Firestone Tire, and others to dismantle dozens of electric transit systems throughout the country, including the $100 million Pacific Electric system. "To preclude the return of electric vehicles to the dozens of cities it motorized, GM extracted from the local transit companies contracts which prohibited their purchase of '. . . any new equipment using any fuel or means of propulsion other than gas.' "[29]

Another example of the application of economic power was provided by the international energy crisis of 1973–74. There can be little doubt that it was in good part instigated by the oil giants, as well as the Arab states. Secret memoranda indicated that prior to the

Arab oil embargo, Aramco, the consortium run by Exxon, Mobil, Standard of California, and Texaco, had been trying to influence the Saudi Arabian government to raise oil prices.[30] Economists for the participating companies figured that by buying oil from the Arab countries at a higher price—by buying dear and selling dear—their profits could be greatly increased. The reasons were simple. The inelasticity of demand for energy, especially gasoline, allowed the companies to raise prices to consumers in proportion to increased costs—thus raising the absolute volume of profits and the rate of return on invested capital. For the oil which these companies produced domestically, the whole of the full increase in the sale price would accrue as a net gain.

During the energy crisis the machinations of the oil giants seemed to be shrouded in an air of conspiracy. There were persistent rumors that at the very time the motorists' tanks were running dry, gasoline storage tanks were full to the brim. In fact, it was impossible to get accurate statistics on storage capacities and fuel reserves from the energy giants.[31] While long lines formed at the fuel pumps, and prices for fuel and heating oil zoomed upward, the public was told to accept the fact that oil wells were being shut down due to poor profitability.[32]

9

The Last Great Merger

There has arisen, quite apart from the ordinary operations of the state, a government of industry which in its own distinctive way has its constitution and its statutes, its administrative and judicial processes, and its own manner of dealing with those who do not abide by the law of the industry.

Walton Hamilton

Yet the whole scheme could not have been carried off without government compliance or passivity. A Federal Energy Office was set up which seemed to be more intent on keeping public opinion and Congress in line than in regulating the industry or protecting energy consumers. The Office echoed industry propaganda that if fuel prices were not allowed to skyrocket (à la the "free market"), production would be discouraged and shortages would become more critical. Elsewhere in the Nixon Administration fuel company executives coordinated government policies from strategic locations within the Defense and Interior departments.[1] If that were not enough to assure a field day for the powerful and profit-hungry industry, the Nixon Administration announced that it would draft hundreds of oil executives into government service in order to administer the regulation of their own industry, while the House and Senate introduced "energy emergency" bills that suspended or limited operations of antitrust laws in the interest of solving the energy shortage.[2] The Administration led a full-scale attack on environmental restraints, rammed the Alaskan Pipeline Bill through Congress,[3] and promised to veto any legislation that might restrict industry profits.[4] The Energy Office and the Cost of Living Council meanwhile issued dubious regulatory decrees which allowed the oil industry to net billions of dollars of added revenue.[5]

While the public was being fleeced, oil company ads and government propaganda turned the issues away from industrial abuses to the sins of consumption. Christmas tree lights were turned off. Congress staged portentous debates on the merits of standard versus daylight time, and passed a law imposing a 55 mph speed limit on the nation's highways.

Similar political maneuvers were being carried out in other countries, if only on a smaller scale. A major scandal broke out in Italy when it was discovered that the oil industry had engaged in widespread bribery of politicians in nearly every major party.[6] In Japan, one of the hardest-hit industrial nations, oil executives sat with their heads bowed as the legislature probed allegations of political corruption and conspiracy.[7]

The "energy crisis" illustrates how it is impossible to speak of the economic effects of the centralization of capital apart from its political effects. In theory, the oil corporations should be nothing more than impartial participants in the political-economic scene, governed by the technical exigencies of the marketplace. In reality, they constitute a sovereign political authority more powerful than many of the world's nation-states. Over the years they have distilled a potent mix of economic power and political leverage. They have their own councils, spies, research, and planning. They have the ability to enter into and enforce treaties in the form of contracts, agreements, and consortia for the production, distribution, and sale of their products. They mount powerful public relations and lobbying campaigns to secure the remaining political-economic gains (tax breaks, import quotas, research subsidies) not ceded to them by law.[8] Most important of all, government itself is deeply involved in their campaign to secure a strategic vantage over the world economy.

Thus the tactical maneuvers of big business are inseparably bound up with a strategy of political control. The natural extension of the principle of competition under modern conditions is the attempt not only to capture the commanding heights of the economy, but also to gain a secure and decisive influence in political circles.

The interplay between business and government was again highlighted during the natural gas shortage during the winter of 1976–1977. As schools and factories were being closed in seventeen states east of the Rocky Mountains, many of the same companies that brought us the oil crisis were spending millions of dollars to convince us that their natural gas business was being driven to bankruptcy by federal price controls. Their reserves were running out, and without higher prices they could not afford to explore for more. Even the Federal Power Commission and the Federal Energy Administration, two of the agencies which are supposed to oversee the industry, joined in the lobbying for deregulation.

Unfortunately, the only source of data on what the nation's "proved" (certain) natural gas reserves are is the industry itself. Once a year the gas producers' trade group, the American Gas Association (AGA), conducts a secret poll of its members to determine this all-important figure. Curiously, beginning in 1968 the AGA found that consumption was exceeding new discoveries, causing proved reserves to shrink. Curious, because that was the year in which the Supreme Court ruled "that the FPC could let producers increase the price of gas whenever AGA's figures showed that their rate of new discoveries had decreased."[9]

Despite the terrible oppressions of government controls, the natural-gas producers have managed to triple prices in just over three years. In 1972 the price of gas sold to interstate pipelines was 21.69 cents per 1,000 cubic feet; by August 1976 it was 65.27 cents.[10] At the same time, the volume of gas sold in interstate commerce dropped from 24 trillion cubic feet to 21 trillion, hardly the expected response from the competitive market the industry is always braying about—unless gas reserves were truly falling rapidly, in which case complete deregulation would seem to be the quickest way to use up what precious little remains.

The telephone industry is another in which corporate power seeks to usurp political power for its own monopolistic purposes. The American Telephone and Telegraph Company reported spending $1,040,009 in the second quarter of 1976 alone to convince the U.S. Congress to strengthen the company's monopoly privileges:

> According to the trade association for independent [AT&T allied] telephone companies, "legislative committees have been formed in each of the 50 states to coordinate efforts to secure sponsorship of the legislation, launch educational and media programs, and develop grass roots support." Included in that effort are canned editorials, "moderate in tone," distributed to local newspapers, stock speeches for telephone executives to give in their hometowns, bill-stuffer brochures titled, "Contrived Competition Means Higher Telephone Rates," and AT&T-financed debates before local "opinion leaders."[11]

AT&T's bill before Congress, modestly entitled the Consumer Communications Reform Act, would outlaw competition in the growing field of private business communications and terminal equipment. One unique provision: the bill would even exempt AT&T from antitrust suits, so it could buy up its outlawed competitors.[12]

While few industries match the energy giants or AT&T for size, many other illustrations could be used to show that the joint exercise of economic and political power is the rule, not the exception, in the era of big business.

This is not the way it happens in the textbooks. The liberal economic ideology commands a "good government" not to ally itself with special interests, but to "give all its aid in such a shape as to encourage and nurture any rudiments it may find of a spirit of individual exertion."[13]

This aid was only for the sake of expediency, not to interfere with the general principle of laissez faire. Government was only to undertake infrastructure-type tasks such as national defense and the administration of justice, which private interest could not be relied upon to do. John Stuart Mill noted that there were:

> . . . a multitude of cases in which governments, with general approbation, assume powers and execute functions for which no reason can be assigned except the simple one, that they conduce to general convenience. We may take as an example, the function (which is a monopoly too) of coining money. This is assumed for no more recondite purpose than that of saving to individuals the trouble, delay, and expense of weighing and assaying. No one, however, even of those most jealous of state interference, has objected to this as an improper exercise of the powers of government. Prescribing a set of standard weights and measures is another instance. Paving, lighting, and cleansing the streets and thoroughfares, is another; whether done by the general government, or as is more usual, and generally more advisable, by a municipal authority. Making or improving harbours, building lighthouses, making surveys in order to have accurate maps and charts, raising dykes to keep the sea out, and embankments to keep rivers in, are cases in point.[14]

Inasmuch as the nature of these functions, and the manner in which monies are raised for their execution, is determined by the political process, politics must inevitably intrude upon economics. But providing basic support for the national economy is not the same as aiding particular interests. Economists still conceive of government as acting in a technical-scientific capacity, not a political one. Outside of specialized concerns of welfare theory or antitrust, the question of political-economic power is most conspicuous by its absence. The only political problem is to persuade the politicians to carry out the right policies and administer the prescribed doses of economic medicine.[15]

In the modern institutional setting, we are faced with an increasing politicization of pricing and demand. The centralization of private power causes government to move to center stage, not just to perform Keynesian manipulations but to act as the medium for regulatory decisions affecting the operating details of every significant industry in the economy. Not that government is the handmaiden to big business. When giant corporations are governments in and of themselves, it is incumbent on government to prevent rival vested interests from putting a mutual stranglehold on the economy. In effect, government regulation is necessary for the maintenance of monopoly control. Capitalism today cannot be prudently managed without government intervention, from aggregate fiscal and monetary affairs down to the laboriously petty details of business enterprise.

Of course the rise of consolidated economic interests is just one of the reasons why government has played an increasingly important role in the economy. The market is completely unsuited to many of the tasks of coordinating a complex technological and urban society. Commercial radio and television would be impossible without FCC controls. The maintenance of a credit economy would be unthinkable without the Federal Reserve or the SEC. The automobile would be useless without government streets, highways, bridges, and tunnels. There would be few trained workers or managers without public education. For the multinational corporation, the marines and the CIA are often more valuable than trade fairs or market research. Now for the sake of capital's future, government must become actively involved in resource preservation and environmental management.

Newspapers are full of examples of the convergence of economic and political processes. During a single week (May 12–18, 1974), there were no less than 209 illustrations to be found in the pages of the *New York Times, New York Post, Wall Street Journal,* and *National Observer.* These ranged from a decision by the governor of New York to back state aid to the Con Ed Company, to new federal factory standards which would limit workers' exposure to vinyl chloride, to the disclosure that a Texas congressman was working to pass measures that would allow hundreds of thousands of new billboards on the nation's highways.

The following chart on the Joint National Enterprise is intended to illustrate more concretely the degree to which the public domain has enlarged and become effectively merged with the private domain.

Each industry in the economy is shown in accordance with its share of the nation's employment. The vertical axis shows, on a scale of zero to ten, the intensity of government involvement in industry.

Such a scale is necessarily inexact, as it is impossible to know precisely the effect of a tariff on imported cars or safety inspections in the coal mines. In addition to the government sphere itself (Social Security, Amtrak, schools, and police), government involvement in private enterprise takes many forms. These include licensing, price regulation, special taxes (or loopholes) and tariffs, government purchase and finance, research funding, product standards, health codes, and pollution controls. The chart is designed to display, roughly, the combined impact of various measures on each industry. (Every industry is represented, though space does not permit each to be labeled.)

We are only trying to measure the particular and direct, not the general, effects of government. We count write-offs for "intangible drilling expenses" but not the capital gains tax credit, even though the latter favors capital-intensive industries above labor-intensive ones. Government spending and transfers have an important indirect impact on most industries (as a rule they account for 10 percent or so of total sales[16]), but only direct government purchase and finance are reflected in our chart. Similarly, no attempt has been made to include government fiscal policy or foreign military aid.

Even with such a rough sketch as this it is easy to see that the realm of laissez faire has been relegated, by and large, to the subsidiary manufacturing, trade, and service industries that have little strategic bearing on the economy as a whole. This sphere, in which government has only a minor direct impact (2 or less on our scale), comprises little more than four tenths of the total employment. At the other end of the scale, nearly two tenths of those employed are on government payrolls.[17] Evidently, those functions which it has been found convenient for government to assume are indeed considerable. The in-between four tenths of the work force is engaged by private firms with strong ties to government. Most "big business" falls under this category; for instance, auto manufacturers, banks, petroleum companies, and electric utilities. In such industries, lawmaking is as important as pricemaking. Reasonable and responsible business management requires that close attention be given to the cultivation of government aid and cooperation.

The Joint National Enterprise

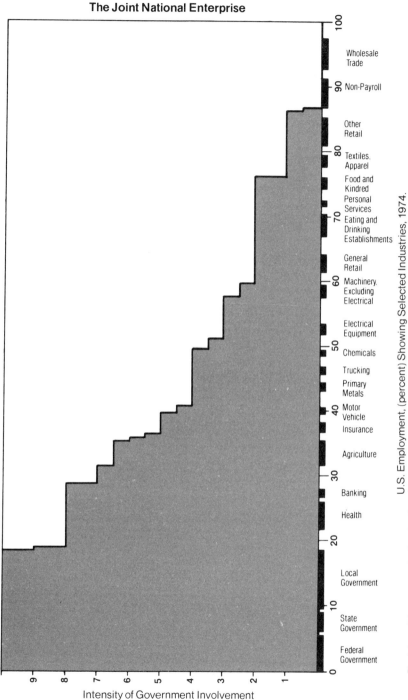

U.S. Employment, (percent) Showing Selected Industries, 1974.

The laissez-faire economy is almost extinct. Few workers are employed in industries not directly affected by government. The manufacturing, trade, and service industries in which government has little or no direct impact (2 or less on our scale) comprise little more than four tenths of the total employment. At the other end of the scale, nearly two tenths of all workers are on government payrolls. The in-between four tenths of the work force is engaged by auto manufacturers, banks, petroleum companies, electric utilities, and other private firms with strong government ties.

Thus the evolution of business and technology have transformed the laissez-faire economy. The decision processes of industry and finance have become more centralized, often within government itself. Through the evolution of law and custom, the executive, legislative, or judicial branches of government have become increasingly involved with business, often through the creation of tailor-made regulatory agencies combining all three functions.

We are witnessing, in effect, the Last Great Merger: the merger of the economic and political systems. The process has not been advertised—except through the customary and misleading conservative attacks on big government—as it runs counter to the traditional notion of the separation of state and economy. Politicians and business leaders are not likely to pose, at least in public, as members of the board of directors of a merged establishment.

In a broad sense, business has always been the business of the modern state. As Veblen aptly expressed it, " . . . it is the national establishment that gives effect to the code of natural rights in this modern scheme of things. The two together make the framework of democratic institutions."[18] And as anyone who reads Charles A. Beard's seminal study will discover, the drafting of the American Constitution provided a remarkable view of how this political-economic framework is put together.[19] Ever since that day, the American National Establishment has been handing out grants of land and money, erecting tariff barriers, and charging up San Juan Hill in its mission to extend and protect the rights of capital.

As the laissez-faire era draws to a close, this relationship between business and politics becomes more involved and intense. Back in the 1930s, studies were done which revealed a pattern of interlocking control between seemingly independent private corporations. It would be appropriate now to extend this analysis to include the complex web of interlocks between industry and government. It would be likely to show that, for most practical purposes, state power and private capital have been consolidated into a Joint National Enterprise.

Part 3
THE FADING IDEAL

10

Growth . . .
and Decay

It must always have been seen, more or less distinctly, by political economists, that the increase of wealth is not boundless: that
at the end of what they term the progressive state lies the stationary state, that all progress in wealth is but a postponement of
this, and that each step in advance is an approach to it.

John Stuart Mill

Off and on throughout the history of political economy theorists
have been intrigued with the notion of the stationary state. Indeed,
one must wonder about the future of any system of political economy
which is fundamentally based upon the process of capital accumulation and expansion. What technical adjustments occur as development unfolds? Is there some source of limitless growth, or will the
well run dry? If it does, what then?

The economists who have tackled these questions often rejected
out of hand any idea that capital could be a perpetually expanding
force. Instead of assuming that capitalist growth would go on for-
ever, they wanted to know when and how it was going to wind down.
Adam Smith himself believed that once a country had acquired its
"full complement of riches," both wages and profits would probably
be depressed.[1] This idea was elaborated by David Ricardo, who
believed that the limit to agricultural output constituted a natural
barrier to industrial expansion:

There cannot . . . be accumulated in a country any amount of capital
which cannot be employed productively, until wages rise so high in
consequence of the rise of necessaries, and so little consequently remains for the profits of stock, that the motive for accumulation
ceases.[2]

As capital accumulated and population grew, Ricardo reasoned, poorer and poorer lands would be brought under cultivation. Since the prices of produce had to be high enough to bring the last acres of marginal land into cultivation, these prices would rise as worse soils were employed. The owners of the better lands would benefit from the rise in prices, since they would be able to charge higher rents. Wages would also rise, but only as a consequence of the rising prices of necessities, not because of a rise in the workers' standard of consumption. (If anything, they would be worse off than before.)

Capitalists would be in the worst position. As marginal productivity fell in agriculture, rising rents and wages would eat into the volume of profit. Eventually the rate of profit would sink so low that it no longer would pay to invest, and growth would stop. Ricardo's demonstration that the self-contained capitalist nation provided a limited field for industrial expansion provided a strong argument for colonization and unrestricted agricultural imports. Nevertheless, even if capitalism became a world system, it would eventually reach its limits.

John Stuart Mill regarded this prospect with more equanimity than most. In his famous chapter on the stationary state, he even looked forward to the day when men were no longer preoccupied with "struggling to get on." At last people might turn their attentions from cultivating wealth to cultivating the Art of Living and elevating the universal lot.[3] Keynes, too, foresaw the day when those still addicted to the money-making passion would have to be content to play the game for lower stakes.[4]

Surprisingly enough, capital's most severe critics did not think that the system was doomed because there were natural industrial limits. At the risk of oversimplifying their views, they took infinite industrial progress for granted, independent of the particular system of productive relations in force at the moment. Capital was destined to go, not because the progress it had set in motion was due to end, but because it would come to stand in the way of its continuation.

The most formidable exponent of this viewpoint was, of course, Karl Marx. Although he flirted with classical arguments of industrial limits with his discovery of "The Law of the Tendency of the Rate of Profit to Fall,"[5] his principal theme emphasized the growing antagonism between the forces of production set in motion by capital and their limited productive and distributive relations. Industrial progress would eventually reach the point where the old order is too confining.

It might seem surprising that conservative economists were the ones more likely to emphasize industrial limits. Of course they were using this as an argument against confining capital within national boundaries. Then, too, if growth was not perpetual, no criticism of the capitalist order was implied, even though that order might have to undergo a transformation as the industrial limit was approached.

The notion of a physical limit to accumulation was a less tenable one for capital's critics. They did not need to show that growth could be perpetual, but they certainly strengthened their argument by maintaining that the main barriers to growth in the historical present were social rather than natural. It enabled them to demonstrate a tension between industrial and social processes that pointed to the possibility of a radical break. The old order would give way to a higher one which transcended the existing limits to production.

More contemporary economists have tended to be strongly expansionist, regardless of their political leanings. The theories of two eminent American political economists are especially interesting, not only for their contrasting viewpoints but because both thought that technological progress would be the death of capital. The conservative Schumpeter had a unique argument which he pursued with rigorous, if somewhat simplistic, logic. The other, Thorstein Veblen, developed Marx's theory—with a flair and genius that has not been equaled since—in light of modern capitalist, especially American, experience through the early part of the twentieth century.

Schumpeter had spent many years pondering capitalism's course, culminating with the publication of his *Capitalism, Socialism and Democracy* in 1942. In this work he questioned what would happen if methods of production reached such a state of perfection that they would admit no further improvement:

> A more or less stationary state would ensue. Capitalism, being essentially an evolutionary process, would become atrophic. There would be nothing left for entrepreneurs to do. They would find themselves in much the same situation as generals would in a society perfectly sure of permanent peace. Profits and along with profits the rate of interest would converge toward zero. The bourgeois strata that live on profits and interest would tend to disappear. The management of industry and trade would become a matter of current administration, and the personnel would unavoidably acquire the characteristics of a bureaucracy. Socialism of a very sober type would almost automatically come into being. Human energy would turn away from business. Other than economic pursuits would attract the brains and provide the adventure.[6]

Schumpeter believed that there was no danger that technological perfection would occur, ending economic growth, in the near future. Yet he believed that it was but a short step from this hypothetical peril to a more imminent concern: that the entrepreneur's function of revolutionizing the methods of production would become so routinized and bureaucratized that the certainty of productive improvements would eliminate risk, and render profit obsolete. This reduction of innovation to a routine was almost as bad, from the point of view of the capitalist, as the elimination of technological progress itself:

> Since capitalist enterprise, by its very achievements, tends to automatize progress, we conclude that it tends to make itself superfluous—to break to pieces under the pressure of its own success. The perfectly bureaucratized giant industrial unit not only ousts the small- or medium-sized firm and "expropriates" its owners, but in the end it also ousts the entrepreneur and expropriates the bourgeoisie as a class which in the process stands to lose not only its income but also what is infinitely more important, its function.[7]

By this reasoning, Schumpeter arrived at the startling and paradoxical conclusion that "capitalism is being killed by its achievements." The end of capital was not the stationary state of Mill or the institutional breakdown of Marx, but a bureaucratized state of perpetual industrial achievement.

His argument has a basic flaw, in that it rests upon the belief that entrepreneurship is the main source of profit, even under monopoly: he saw profits as the reward for the managerial acumen that goes into making and marketing a better or cheaper product. This contrasts with Marx's (correct) view that profits arise out of the capitalists' monopoly of the means of production and their ability to control and exploit the laborers. Still, Schumpeter had a point. Wealth holders might still clip their coupons, but capital would no longer serve any function once its creative and proprietary aspects were divorced.

Thorstein Veblen also seemed to deny that the price system any longer played a role in promoting industrial efficiency. He drew a careful distinction between industry (the process of producing goods), and business enterprise (the strategic pursuit of pecuniary gain). The modern scheme of industry had worked profound changes in the capitalist's role, rendering him superfluous. The growth of industry, if left to the technicians, would progress in a matter-of-fact, orderly fashion. Economic growth was an impersonal process of "technical balancing and articulation" proceeding on the basis of scientific logic in accordance with established principles of physics and chemistry. The engineers and skilled technical workers were the paramount factors of industrial progress.

Industry, according to Veblen, had no use for business; the mechanical system had no need of the price system. The captains of industry who sought to turn technological resources to new uses and larger efficiency were a vanishing trade. These adventurers who combined industry with business had risen to prominence in "that era of (temperately) free competition that lies between the Industrial Revolution of the eighteenth century and the rise of corporation finance in the nineteenth." They had no place in the new institutional order.[8]

Veblen and Schumpeter agreed that industry had settled into something of an orderly routine. Progress itself had taken on an everyday, impersonal character of material cause and effect. Likewise, they both concluded that the capitalist had lost his creative (entrepreneurial) function and had become an anachronism on the modern institutional scene.

Beyond this point, they parted company. Schumpeter saw the bourgeoisie being reduced to wage earners, although he expected they might hang around for some time, collecting "quasi-rents and monopoloid gains." From Veblen's viewpoint, Schumpeter was standing capitalist society on its head. Ours was a business culture, governed by business values which directed industry toward business ends. And the end toward which business strove was the maximum pecuniary net gain, not industrial growth.

To Veblen the technicians and the businessmen had become "the conjugate foci of the economic system" about which "the orbit of the economic world now swings." And as the industrial arts became "an increasingly intricate and exacting network of give and take," the two foci would draw further apart. The business principles governing the nation's economic life—principles of salesmanship, credit, and sabotage—would become increasingly at odds with the industrial system until the point would be reached at which the "systematic retardation and derangement of productive industry which is entailed by the current businesslike management will work out in a progressive abatement of the margin of net output of the industrial system at large."[9] Business, in short, was the enemy of industrial progress.

Veblen based his argument upon the realities of the administered price system and its institutions of monopoly, salesmanship, and credit. He showed how the prevailing business principles affected the industrial system. Schumpeter, on the other hand, argued as if capitalist economy is governed by industrial means and ends. He thought of corporations as no more than mechanical instruments for putting society's demands into material form. If they could function just as well without their owners, capitalists, along with their profits, would "atrophy" out of existence. Somehow.

Thus Schumpeter and Veblen agreed that the old competitive dynamic was dead and that capitalists had outlived their industrial usefulness. Schumpeter, with his false notion of profit, thought the capitalists would simply fade away. Veblen's argument closely followed Marx's social-political scenario for class conflict. Once industry, for all practical purposes, was in the hands of technicians and workers, they might tire of seeing their work sabotaged, and themselves exploited by a minority class that had no visibly useful function. As the derangement of industry passed the point of no return, the technicians and workers would almost be forced to take over. Capital would be overthrown, not because it failed to generate profits, but because it had become a roadblock to industrial progress.

It is interesting that Schumpeter and Veblen both saw the industrial economy as a rational system on its own, either superficially connected with market incentives and controls, or totally at variance with pecuniary motive. This faith in industrial rationality was a critical weakness in their arguments, for they did not recognize the role market mechanisms play in regulating the industrial system. They placed too much reliance on the "aimless dynamism," as Lewis Mumford called it, of a modern industrial and scientific culture. They assumed that a complex industrial order could be sensibly governed through the autonomous decisions of industrial bureaucrats, or by a community of engineers and workmen acting in accordance with broader, but still self-evident principles.

But while this belief that capitalists were becoming superfluous or counterproductive was a break with the classical tradition, the belief in industrial rationality was not. In a way, the competitive theory of markets serves as a cloak for the classical faith in industrial harmony. It rests on the tenuous equation of industrial drives with social need, mechanism with purpose. In this respect, the competitive theorists were on no firmer ground than the technocratic sands of Schumpeter and Veblen.

This faith in industrial progress is clearly behind the ideal of growth. As nature abhors a vacuum, economists abhor a stationary state. For a long time growth and progress have been synonymous terms, and in the United States especially, the capitalist economy and its vigorous expansion has long been identified with the national interests.

John Stuart Mill not withstanding, it is almost universally believed that the cessation of growth would have dire consequences for the political stability and economic viability of the capitalist system. For a system of institutionalized inequality and conflict, a continuous "growth dividend" is essential to buy civil peace and pay for other needs not met by the private market. Growth is the reliever for the tensions of poverty and discrimination.

But what is this "growth"? More? More what?

The traditional viewpoint (though rarely stated, since economists rarely realize their bias) is that the quality of life is primarily determined by the output of the consumer goods sector of the economy. Little thought is given to personal services, especially when they are not profit-making. As increasing numbers of women enter the work force, that is a pure gain from the economist's point of view. Their household chores never counted in the GNP—presumably housewives are easily replaced by dishwashers, TV dinners, and other convenience goods.

Servants are for the rich. Most of the services consumed by the lower and middle classes are tied to the process of earning a living rather than serving as a direct source of consumer satisfaction. Child care, dry cleaning, employment agencies, business schools, banking, and public transport are all, to a greater or lesser extent, forms of spending and investment that do not yield any net increase in "consumer satisfaction," as that term is generally construed. Also, those services most conducive to personal health and enjoyment are among those least subject to productivity improvements. Included here would be medical care, haircutting, public gardens and parks, museums, theaters, orchestras, and restaurants.

Now that day-care centers are closing, museums and libraries are on short hours, and neither milkmen nor doctors make house calls, we see that it has been for good reason that economists have looked toward expansion of the consumer goods sector, not services, as the means of raising the standard of living under capitalism. By and large they have not been disappointed. Modern invention and mass production techniques have brought certain kinds of consumer satisfaction within the reach of many individuals in the lower and middle income groups. Since butlers and formal gardens do not come off an assembly line, mass production has an undoubted egalitarian bent.

Indeed, it is irrefutable fact that Louis XIV did not have a decently equipped dentist (which he sorely needed), a transistor radio, a roll-on antiperspirant, a sports car, or an electric blanket. What praise would be too great for that engine of capitalist progress which, in many material respects, makes every man a king!

Even in Edwardian England capitalism had still not achieved the full mass-production munificence of the latter-day American variety. There the middle, professional class was a relatively small segment of society. Even its more humble members were comparatively rich and could afford a servant or two. Since then, the masters have derived fewer benefits from the growth of mass production than the servants. From the utilitarian standpoint, that is good, since the members of society on the bottom rungs of the economic ladder are those who, theoretically, have the most to gain. In accordance with the hedonistic calculus of classical economy, egalitarianism is the means to achieving optimum utility, assuming that all human beings (economic men) have the same basic wants and drives. It is altogether fitting that an increased level of general welfare is achieved at the expense of a relative decline in personal services, particularly for the upper strata of society.

Of course, we must always remember that the classical theory of utility is based upon scarcity of products and the insatiability of demand. People will always want more than can be produced. As production increases, as per capita consumption reaches higher and higher levels, the actual psychic satisfaction derived from each increment of production may diminish. If production in this country were doubled overnight, it would certainly not double the satisfaction people derive from consumption. To the extent that this satisfaction is gained by the invidious comparison of one's lot with one's neighbor's, an increase in output yields no net increase in utility.

Whatever its psychic utilitarian limits, many of the benefits of mass production are real enough. But what are the implications of this continual expansion of the output of goods? If capitalist growth is based upon the goods-producing, as opposed to the service-producing, sector of the economy, important changes are likely to occur, in time, in the industrial structure.

To see what happens, let us first try to establish the nature of the technical link between the growing output of consumer products and the intermediate goods and services used in producing them. In a mature capitalist economy these intermediate products include not only private capital's energy, raw materials, factories, machines, truckers, offices, computers, advertising executives, and bank guards, but an elaborate government-based infrastructure of roads, harbors, police, aircraft carriers, and tax collectors.

Final products are the sole source of ultimate utility. Intermediate products, the capital and infrastructure, are the (presumably) necessary means for producing them. Inasmuch as the intermediate products are inputs to the consumer goods sector, the output of intermediate products must keep pace with the increasing production of consumer goods.

But can productivity gains in the intermediate product sectors of the economy match those in the sector producing consumer goods? If they do not, an increasing proportion of society's resources will be channeled into the intermediate sectors; the capacity to expand will decline and the rate of economic growth will wind down.

Let us look at what occurs when the output of refrigerators, lamps, meats, or vegetables is increased. More raw materials will be used: more steel, glass, feeds, and fertilizers. More transport services will be needed. More warehouse and shelf space will be required to bring the products to the consumer. Similarly, if the rate of homebuilding is increased, more building materials, roads, street cleaners, traffic police, grass seed, fire protection, and tax assessors will be required. More cars will demand more gasoline, more mechanics, insurance agents, and scrap dealers. More airplanes need more magnesium, rubber, and upholstery to be built and more airports, jet fuel, travel agents, airplane mechanics, ticket clerks, air traffic controllers, baggage handlers, and FAA officials to get them off the ground.

Since modern industry found much of its impetus and organizational forms in the development of the military, a martial analogy would be particularly appropriate here. In a modern war every soldier sent to the front must have a multilevel organization behind him. First there is the engineering corps, field communications, nursing, mess and supply, and front line command.

A second line backs up the front. There are a host of "support services" such as transport and supply, maintenance, intelligence, police, construction, medical care, sanitation, training . . . not to mention those engaged in feeding and supplying *these* people.

Then comes the officer corps with their orderlies and support services. And all the civilian advisors, construction firms, airlines, spies, and officials. Plus all the members of the "host" government and their families who have to be properly looked after.

Then there are the "folks back home"—all those engaged in manufacturing the trucks, bombs, clothing, tents, shovels, food, radios . . . even the pencils and paper required for the war effort. Not to forget the fertilizer, raw materials, machinery, transportation, and bookkeeping needed to keep *this* manufacture going.

Last but not least, there are all the greater or lesser "commanders-in-chief" directing the whole operation—all those Pentagon, executive, and legislative officials, along with their advisors, spies, clerks, and so on. With honorable mention, of course, to the American Legion and like patriotic and business organizations, as well as to the agents, police, committees, judges, and jailers who look after those not caught up in the spirit of collective effort.

It is a rare soldier indeed who appreciates all the effort and sacrifice that goes into putting him on the front line!

The same principles apply whether one is fighting a war or putting goods into the hands of consumers. In either case, the supporting array of productive forces is much greater than meets the unappreciative eye. And the larger the required intermediate sectors in relation to the final production stage, be it for the delivery of bombs or automobiles, the greater will be the effect of productivity changes in those sectors upon the ability to deliver final products.

Now it becomes clear why the question of whether productivity in the intermediate sectors keeps pace with that in the consumer goods sector is of such importance. If it falls behind, a larger and larger portion of the total economic effort will be bogged down in producing intermediate outputs.

There are several reasons for believing that intermediate productivity will not keep pace with that of the consumer goods sector— that as time goes on, an increasing proportion of society's total productive effort must be devoted to intermediate products.

One reason is that the output of final goods has drawn on increasing quantities of raw material and intermediate products. Modern agricultural practices use enormous quantities of water, chemical fertilizers, and insecticides. And as great as the increase in industrial output has been, the use of energy to produce this output has risen faster. That is to say, the delivery of intermediate products, such as fertilizers and energy, has had to at least keep pace with the output of final goods.

But as farmlands are turned into suburban developments and as supplies of phosphate, petroleum, timber, copper, tin, and zinc run out, inferior or less accessible reserves will have to be tapped. This means that an increasing amount of labor and capital (and raw materials!) will have to be used to supply the same amount of raw materials or intermediate goods to the consumer goods sector. Tertiary methods of petroleum recovery, for example, require approximately 500,000 pounds of detergent per acre. And the detergent itself is a product of petrochemical feedstock.[10]

A second reason for the relative growth of intermediate employment is that since the intermediate sectors are in considerable part composed of service employment (letter carriers, mechanics, government inspectors, police officers, service station attendants), it is not likely that labor productivity in the intermediate sectors will keep pace with increases in the consumer-goods-producing industries. Thus to keep both sectors expanding at the same rate, employment would have to shift out of the consumer goods sector and into the less productive intermediate sectors.

Nor are these reasons the only grounds on which we can expect to see a shift of employment away from the goods sector and into the intermediate sectors. Going back to our criticism of the classical system we find that:

(1) As new technologies are devised for the purpose of cheapening production and escaping resource limitations, the earth's ecology is upset by the resulting pollution and disruption, and a huge bionomic debt is built up. The effort required to control and correct the damage means that more employment must be put into the intermediate sectors.

(2) A large proportion of resources and productive effort is wasted by suburban sprawl and urban decay. Suburban communities are poor land users and create inefficient transportation patterns. Many cities have entered a vicious cycle of decay involving the destruction of housing, the flight of business, and mounting welfare costs.

(3) Another large chunk of the economic effort has been diverted to the maintenance of law and order. In addition to the police and spies employed by all levels of government, there is a growing force of private police now estimated to total upwards of 400,000 persons.[11] Right behind the spies and police stands a large army of lawyers, accountants, Internal Revenue agents, management consultants, foremen, locksmiths, supervisors, adjusters, auditors, and inspectors called upon because the hedonistic calculus is not always conducive to economic order. Moreover, this vital, if nonproductive, sector is not very susceptible to mechanization.

It scarcely needs to be mentioned that this law-and-order problem is not confined within the nation's borders. "National defense" ex-penditures of upward of $100 billion per year are deemed necessary to maintain a stable multinational economy. (It is presumed that these expenditures are not for the purpose of internal control.) For-eign aid and intelligence, the underwriting of political parties, trade unions, and officials abroad, as well as other miscellaneous expendi-tures are made to keep the bonds of the international competitive order.

It is, of course, hard to measure the effectiveness of such expendi-tures from a cost-benefit point of view. Many economists, among whom Seymour Melman is of note, have argued that it would have been better to spend the money elsewhere. Nevertheless, the anarchic or revolutionary processes which they are supposed to arrest are real enough, and growing. Whether the expenditures are effective, or even counterproductive, these "peacekeeping" efforts are very large, both domestically and internationally.

(4) The growth of monopoly has also tended to divert economic energies away from the production of consumer goods. We saw how many economic decisions have been taken out of the market and put into the hands of a swelling body of corporate and government bureaucrats. Monopolistic, nonprice competition also diverts re-sources and talent into product differentiation, packaging, advertis-ing, and sales.

In sum, it seems fair to guess that the combination of increased material inputs, environmental decay, urban devastation, political anarchy, and monopoly power brings an inevitable constriction of capitalism's growth capacity. These stresses underscore Mill's con-tention that the increase of wealth is not boundless. As capital pro-gresses through more complex and difficult stages, the growth of the intermediate sectors undermines the capacity of the consumer sector. From the rationale of capitalist expansion, this infrastructure shift constitutes a process of structural decay.

Now let us see what has happened to the economy in the postwar period. In the following table we have arranged employment statis-tics in accordance with our sector analysis. This way we can analyze the employment shifts that have occurred, by sector, over the twenty-nine-year period from 1947 to 1975.

The data on payroll employment, when broken down in this way, show that a dramatic restructuring has occurred. Employment in the consumer goods sector fell from 17 million to 11 million, even though total employment was rising. As a proportion of total em-

MILLIONS OF US EMPLOYED, BY SECTOR*

	Consumer Sector			Intermediate Sectors				
	Goods	Services	Total	Goods	Services	Government	Total	Total
1947	17.3	4.6	21.9	9.1	15.3	7.1	31.5	53.4
1950	15.6	4.8	20.4	10.1	15.9	7.7	33.7	54.0
1955	15.6	5.6	21.2	11.3	17.7	9.9	38.9	60.2
1960	14.5	6.6	21.1	11.4	18.9	10.9	41.2	62.2
1965	13.9	8.0	21.9	12.4	20.9	12.8	46.1	67.9
1970	13.4	10.0	23.4	13.4	24.7	15.7	53.8	77.3
1975	11.0	10.9	21.9	14.9	28.8	17.0	60.7	82.5

Sources: *Employment and Earnings* (monthly report); and *Employment and Earnings, United States, 1909–72*, BLS Bulletin 1312–9, U.S. Department of Labor, Bureau of Labor Statistics.

*Payroll employment: the self-employed, private household workers, and family members working without pay are not included.

ployment, the consumer goods sector experienced a 59 percent decline. Intermediate employment rose from 32 million to 61 million, so that nearly three quarters of the nation's workers are now employed in those sectors. Looked at from another angle, intermediate employment was less than double that of consumer goods employment in 1947; by 1975 it was more than five times as great.

Such a shift is remarkable. Allowing that we classified industries arbitrarily[12] and did not account for foreign trade, we can still conclude that a dramatic change has occurred. With three quarters of those employed now working in intermediate industries, the capacity to expand the output of final products appears severely constrained.

In one respect we would expect our data to understate the erosive trend. This is because there is a considerable time lag before the effects of resource depletion and bionomic loss are reflected in structural changes. But now the rising costs of raw materials and farm products and the increasing expenditures on pollution control indicate that these heretofore hidden costs of the post–World War II expansion are catching up with us.

Undoubtedly there are other causes for the postwar shift, especially government spending to prop up the economy. Joan Robinson and other left Keynesians maintain that it was the short-sighted policies of the capitalist state which landed us in the present mess.

Too much has gone into military spending and imperial ventures. Capitalism could shift its resources into the civilian sector; it could meet its own needs for self-preservation while at the same time providing for the long-run needs of the various national populations. At present, however, there is too much narrowness and rigidity:

> Now that the authorities want employment to revive, they can only push industry further down the grooves that it has worn for itself. There is no point in thinking of what we really want, such as abolishing poverty and restoring peace. All we can ask for is what they choose to give us. We must keep the show going or else, we fear, they won't give us anything at all.[13]

Had the policies advocated by the left Keynesians been followed, government would have spent less on military hardware and done more to arrest the decay of the cities and lift the tax burdens of the poor. In this case, the consumer sector may not have fared so badly.

Certainly there is enough productive capacity in the advanced capitalist countries today to more than provide for people's basic needs. If production were properly organized and allocated, we might be freed from acquisitive struggle and be able to direct our thought and energy toward higher pursuits. As Mill said:

> It is scarcely necessary to remark that a stationary condition of capital and population implies no stationary state of human improvement. There would be as much scope as ever for all kinds of mental culture, and moral and social progress; as much room for improving the Art of Living, and much more likelihood of its being improved, when minds ceased to be engrossed by the art of getting on.[14]

Mill had hoped that as society approached a stationary state, it could be organized to promote cultural enrichment and a decent lot for even the lowest classes. His was a bourgeois egalitarian vision. A century later, Keynes gave this view theoretical reinforcement by showing that a more equal distribution of income would raise the aggregate propensity to consume, thereby reducing the level of investment necessary to ensure full employment.

Regrettably, real capitalist decay bears no more resemblance to its imagined idyllic decline than do the technocratic scenarios for its demise of Schumpeter and Veblen. Our present problems will not be solved by an end to growth any more than they have been by its continuation. When growth stops, the economy will still be governed by a predatory alliance of big business and government.

Before, opportunity and innovation were the name of the game.

As the natural order comes apart and there is no growth dividend to play with, everyone turns to the state for help. Bankers, generals, mayors, senators, scientists, public interest advocates—they all see government as the means to either preserving privilege or arresting social decline. The formation of economic goals is now the subject of open political conflict, no longer to be left to the benevolence of the unseen hand of harmonious equilibrium.

11

The Inevitability of Planning

What many will call state planning would, to the average family,
be no more than prudent budgeting.

Felix G. Rohatyn

Felix Rohatyn, the respected investment banker and mastermind
of New York City's financial restructuring, would not have uttered
this charming aphorism even a few years ago. Nor does Paul Sweezy
now draw the contrast he made back in 1942 between a planned
economy and a market one:

> In so far as the allocation of productive activity is brought under
> conscious control, the law of value [which regulates the exchange of
> commodities in a market economy] loses its relevance and impor-
> tance; its place is taken by the principle of planning. In the economics
> of a socialist society the theory of planning should hold the same basic
> position as the theory of value in the economics of a capitalist society.
> Value and planning are as much opposed, and for the same reasons,
> as capitalism and socialism.[1]

How times change! Many East European economists are now
saying that socialist enterprises must heed market values. E. G.
Liberman, a leader of the economic reform movement in the USSR,
thus wrote that in a Socialist economy:

> ... it is essential to reckon with the law of value, and if it becomes
> necessary to violate its demands deliberately, one must know what
> such a violation will cost and how and when this loss will be compen-
> sated.[2]

What "law of value"? Apparently the same law of "commodity
and monetary relations" that operates in a capitalist economy! Liber-

man would not go as far along the road to market socialism as the
Czech economist Ota Šik did in the 1960s,[3] but the abstract "demands" he speaks of are clearly not the conscious decisions of socialist planners.

But lo! See what is happening in America. Jacob Javits, John
Kenneth Galbraith, Henry Ford II, Leonard Woodcock—to name
one representative each from politics, economics, business, and labor
—all tell us we need a planned economy. There are now many
respectable people who would agree with these trenchant words from
Hubert H. Humphrey:

> But make no mistake about it: This economy is already "planned,"
> although not in a rational or coherent way.[4]

Whether the need is for planning, more planning, or better planning, a middle-of-the-road Democrat in America is not supposed to
propose an Economic Planning Board to manage the economy.

Maybe this is all a bad dream . . . or confused semantics. With
socialist economists talking about the law of value and capitalist ones
talking about planning, it is hard to tell who is who nowadays. Are
irreconcilables becoming reconciled? Is the whole world about to
become:

(1) capitalist?

(2) socialist?

(3) one big happy "mixed" economy?

None of the above. The market system is not a panacea for the
problems of a socialist economy. Planning is not an easy way out for
capital. And above all, we are not about to reach the golden compromise combining the best results of the two systems.

Yet the events we are witnessing are not an act of theatre of the
absurd. They are a very real response to some of the profound
difficulties of our day and age. The Eastern European countries have
genuine problems of allocation and motivation for which they may
look, rightly or wrongly, to competitive means to solve. The capitalist countries sense that planning is the only answer to the problems
of population growth, resource use, energy development, and the
urban crisis.

Once the process of decay is understood, the seemingly anomalous
talk of planning under capitalism begins to make sense. We saw that
under present conditions freedom for capital is the surest route to its
destruction. Left to its own devices, capital will lay waste to our
planet, and destroy its initiative and enterprise in the process. Un-

doubtedly some of its supporters see planning as several steps along the road to socialism. But capital's planning for self-preservation is not the same as planning to build socialism. Planning which grows out of revolutionary struggle and democratic initiative is very different from planning to preserve the status quo, even though they may bear some resemblances.

But can capitalists become planners? Schumpeter, for one, wonders aloud whether capital can govern effectively, or even look after its real class interests.

> We have seen that the industrialist and merchant, as far as they are enterpreneurs, also fill a function of leadership. But economic leadership of this type does not readily expand, like the medieval lord's military leadership, into the leadership of nations. On the contrary, the ledger and cost calculations absorb and confine.[5]

When Schumpeter wrote these words, he was concerned about capital's desire to care for, and fight for, its property rights. In that respect, he greatly exaggerated capital's helplessness. But his argument does have relevance when, in the overall interests of capital, the regulation and control of property becomes more important than its defense. Capital may be able to govern a self-regulating society, but it should prove well-nigh impossible to impose even a semirational plan, when that would require the sacrifice of particular vested interests for the sake of the whole.

So as not to subordinate private interest to public purpose, government regulation carefully follows a piecemeal approach. Typically the result is a sort of planning in reverse. The regulated industry, by combining its unity of purpose with the almighty power of the buck, is able to conscript the regulators "into the service of the very interests they were set up to supervise."[6]

There is a tacit acceptance of this new regulatory state among those actively engaged in this joint government-business enterprise. Most notably, government regulators often have an active or latent interest vested in the industries they are appointed to oversee. In seeking US landing rights for the Concorde, it is a matter of accepted and prudent business that the French government should employ the law firm of a former Secretary of State. The British government by chance chose the firm of the first administrator of the Environmental Protection Agency as its counsel. The payrolls of military contractors are loaded with retired generals. FDA officials can be sure of jobs waiting for them with food processors or drug companies when they leave government service. A former chairman of the Federal Communications Commission is today a private lawyer who numbers among his clients CBS, cable television companies, and the American Telephone and Telegraph Company. IBM's battle against a massive antitrust suit brought by the Justice Department is being directed by Nicholas Katzenbach, who—lo and behold—used to be Attorney General.[7] It goes without saying that legislators look after the interests of their constituents, especially if they happen to be major employers or big campaign contributors. The lawmakers are only exercising prudent foresight, since members of Congress who return to the private sector double, on the average, their pregovernment salaries.[8] Such are the rewards of public service!

In early 1974, Congressman Benjamin S. Rosenthal checked into the backgrounds of members of the Federal Energy Office. In response to his request, William E. Simon, who was then administrator of the agency, provided him with a list of 102 employees who had previously worked for the oil industry.[9] Of these, ten held positions of GS-16 or higher and fifty-nine held positions of GS-13 to GS-15. Were these people really expected to take a broad view of the nation's interests?

This question was again raised by a two-year study of nine regulatory agencies prepared by the Oversight Subcommittee of the House Interstate and Foreign Commerce Committee. It found that more than 50 percent of the appointments to regulatory jobs made by the Nixon and Ford administrations were people who had previously served in the regulated industry. The study's conclusion was anticlimactic: that the agencies were more committed to the special interests than they were to the public.[10]

Yet the Federal Reserve System must surely be the envy of all regulatory agencies, from the point of view of special interests. Of the 108 persons who serve on the boards of the twelve Reserve Banks, two thirds, or 72, of the directors are selected by the very banks they are charged with regulating! In five of the 12 districts all formality is dispensed with. Nominations are simply channeled through state bankers' associations, the lobby for the industry.[11] The board of each Reserve Bank selects a president. Five of the presidents (in rotation) serve on the twelve-member Federal Open Market Committee which meets in secret each month to set monetary policy for the entire country. What more could a vested interest ask for?

This sort of regulation is well and good from the point of view of each particular capitalist group. Or even, generally, from the standpoint of the vested interests as a whole vis-à-vis the rest of the population, as in the case of the Federal Reserve perhaps. It fails, and fails miserably, to take care of the long-run class interest of capital when that should conflict with the immediate needs of particular vested groups. In summarizing the long relationship between the oil interests and the government, John Blair was forced to conclude that "the historical role of the federal government has been not to restrain the industry but to make more effective its exploitation of the public interest."[12] But it is not just the public interest that is affected by government oil policies which allow wasteful extraction practices, speed up the depletion of domestic reserves, raise energy costs to industry, undermine the international financial structure, and push poor nations to the brink of bankruptcy.

The failure of government regulation is an important point in understanding the relation between economic decay and the political response. Since the decay process is independent of the general will of capital, government will be forced to act, and in the process there is likely to be some redefinition of the government-business relationship. A strong dose of planning will be thought necessary, not only to correct the faults of the market and to prevent dominant corporations from gaining a stranglehold on the economy, but also to disarm the left and obviate the need for stronger measures of nationalization or control.

In discussing planning, we might as well start by conceding Humphrey's point that a lot of planning is already taking place in the United States.[13] Government budgets run into the hundreds of billions of dollars, practically none of which is spent in accordance with market supply and demand. Some of it, for example price supports and unemployment insurance, deliberately runs counter to the market process.

When the federal government has to choose between the B-1 bomber or more cruise missiles, that is called "planning" and nobody thinks the worse of it. When a census is taken to predict how many schools, hospitals, and boxes of Pampers are needed, the DAR does not bat an eyelash. When the government makes long-range forecasts of resource needs—or, yes, even of the weather!—or when the Federal Reserve decides how fast the money supply should grow, nobody accuses them of destroying capitalism. Even Gerald Ford's "Project Independence," a $100-billion program of government-backed energy research and development—with the goal of making the United States independent of foreign suppliers—received applause from the stalwart champions of free enterprise.

Perhaps the first conscious effort at overall planning in the United States came with the implementation of Keynesian policy: government plans and actions to achieve full employment, stable prices, balanced growth, and so on. This has come to be the accepted way, although it too was denounced as Socialist in its time. Once government and business became sold on Keynes's ideas, it was widely believed that the last barrier to engineering full employment and balanced growth had been removed. The primary dilemma had been how to get western economies out of the depression and keep them out. A secondary problem was that of deciding how the primary goal should be accomplished, whether through corporate aid or social programs. In the atmosphere of cold war imperialism, military contractors and multinational corporations carried off most of the prizes.

Now these policies are found wanting. There is a growing awareness that we are not simply dealing with the problem of periodic crises or depression. The energy shortage, permanent inflation, urban decay, and bankrupt railroads are viewed as symptoms of the inability of Keynesian fiscal and monetary policies to maintain stable prosperity. There is a newly felt need to foresee problems in advance and to concoct specific remedies, which is likely to lead to the establishment of a system of indicative planning for the United States, similar to those of Western Europe and Japan.

This is, basically, Senators Humphrey and Javits's idea of what planning would be like here. Government—Congress and an Economic Planning Board in the Executive Office of the President in this case—assesses national problems and priorities.[14] It draws up a set of national goals, debates and modifies them, then points the way—"indicates"—to government agencies and private business the anticipated levels of government spending, private investment, production, demand, money supply, trade, and so on needed to fulfill the plan. Government urges business (whose leaders cooperated in drawing up the plan) to adjust their own plans to be in consonance with the national one. Flexible taxes, grants, and other inducements can be used to see that this is done. Government can also, as it has in the past, adjust its own fiscal and monetary activity as the private sector performs higher or lower than expected.

The senators claim that their proposed system of planning would "not permit any economic coercion, direct or indirect . . . the Economic Planning Board cannot tell anyone what to do—its powers are those of persuasion—not direction."[15] Were that the case, it would be hard to imagine how such a planning setup would more than marginally affect the environmental, resource, and social concerns raised by the senators. What happens if our planners discover that the banks are not investing enough in inner-city housing, or the energy giants are a threat to the goal of maintaining a competitive economy? What if drastic conservation measures are needed? When private decision-makers do not conform to what the plan considers to be in the long-term national interests, is the plan to be scrapped as being unrealistic? Or do the senators imagine that the government will somehow foot the bill for the difference?

Any remotely rational plan would raise real conflicts between private and public, between short-run and long-run, between big business and small, and to the extent that corporate interests are not mutually intertwined, between competing vested interests.

Thus when bankers and businessmen speak out against planning, they may be voicing real concern that their profit and initiative will be destroyed. But in the absence of a politically strong, well-informed left they have little to fear. Doctors fought vigorously against Medicare and Medicaid, only to profit enormously in the end. In the same manner, the first attempts at planning, even if initially undertaken in response to the wider needs of the system, will end up serving special interests, just as regulation has done in the past.

It must be borne in mind that part of the need for a stronger system of planning stems from the fact that the government now has less, not more, room to maneuver than under the old Keynesian programs. Closing the alliance between big business and government through the economic planning system undermines the competitive market further without offering much in return. Jean Ripert, the French High Commissioner of Planning, readily admits "that even a strong dose of voluntaristic planning will not by itself succeed in providing the public with 'a sense of direction for social change.' All it can do is provide an already existing political leadership with some technical tools to do a better job. . . ."[16] Not a reassuring prospect.

In other words, from the start, capitalist planning must first and foremost be planning to help capital. Any improvement in social conditions will be no more than a fortuitous aftereffect.[17] But will policies to help business really breathe life into the capitalist system?

We can get a good idea of why plans will run amuck if we examine Felix G. Rohatyn's views in support of suggestions to revive the Reconstruction Finance Corporation of the 1930s. The crucial difference this time, according to Rohatyn, is that the RFC will be not just a "last-ditch creditor" but "a first step toward state planning of the economy." The billions it would spend infusing equity into the banks, financing the merger of failing airlines, investing in energy research, and building power plants would have the aim of a "major restructuring for the public purpose."[18]

What goes by the highfalutin phrases of "state planning" and "public purpose" is nothing more than the government "injecting equity capital where none is available in quantity" into private corporations: using the public till as the safety net for business. This time around the RFC will not even bother with such mundane tasks as public works or disaster aid.

State planning is not to encroach on private capital. Should the RFC stumble into some lucrative enterprise that our timid capitalists have overlooked, Rohatyn would insist that it

> ... only remain as an investor, either as a part-owner or creditor, until such time as it can, in the public interest, divest itself of the enterprise in which it invests and this investment is eligible for normal market channels or until the markets are capable of performing their function.[19]

"In the public interest!" This is the same old deal: the public takes the risks; the vested interests get the profits, including, presumably, Rohatyn's own investment bank, Lazard Frères and Company.[20]

What Rohatyn actually wants to do is to politically upgrade the nation's debt structure as businesses fail or investors lose their nerve.

The process works something like this: if private capital wants to put up housing in Manhattan, but does not want to take any risks, New York City is supposed to provide it with tax credits and rent subsidies. If the city's finances are flimsy, investors will look to New York State for backing. The state can set up an agency to build the housing, using bonds that are floated to private banks and investors. If the state's credit turns sour, the federal government can guarantee the state's bonds, perhaps through the new RFC.[21]

The real difference this time is that the new RFC would not be working upon the morass of the 1930s, but upon the decay of the 1970s and beyond. It will not be working in an era of insufficient demand but one in which the entire capitalist system is losing its coherence and direction. By underwriting big business even in the best of times, we would be taking a giant step forward, not toward socialism, but toward state capitalism. Government would be the hired rent collector, and business would be further insulated from the discipline of the market. This time, government would often be the investor of first, as well as last, resort.[22]

Clearly, this type of planning does not lead to rational economy. By further weakening market controls, it diminishes what rationality the controls still retain. To take one of Rohatyn's examples, airlines may fly at a loss because they are expensive and inefficient compared to other forms of transport. By underwriting the airlines as he suggests, government may only be guaranteeing a less efficient economy than the one a market would provide.

More general planning policies than those Rohatyn suggests avoid the appearance of undermining market efficiency. One of the keys to stability in the era of decline is the formation of a "social compact" between business and labor. Both sides agree to make sacrifices in the interests of national recovery, but since the climate must be agreeable before wealth-holders invest or factories produce, the brunt of the bargain must fall on the workers.

Britain's wage controls or the wage and price controls Nixon sprung on the economy in 1971 can be effective, if heavy-handed, methods of enforcing the social compact. More subtle means of redistribution are preferred, such as the use of tax reductions as a stimulus to investment. An important reason why Keynesian policies were so readily accepted is that lower tax rates and accelerated depreciation allowances have narrowed the slice of tax revenue coming from corporate income taxes from 23 percent in 1950 to 14 percent in 1974.[23] We can expect this trend to continue although it has an obvious limit. It is well known that already some highly profitable corporations pay little or no taxes at all to the federal government. Also, the widespread belief that the American tax system is highly progressive (that the rich pay much higher tax rates than the poor) is notoriously at variance with the facts. The growing number of loopholes and exemptions for the rich, together with an increasing reliance on Social Security and sales taxes (which fall more heavily on low-income groups) have effectively destroyed progressive taxation. Today the US tax system is proportional overall —all income groups are taxed at roughly the same rate.[24]

But why stop at taxes? The other side to taxation is government spending. When the economy gets tight, capital steps up its attack on programs to provide schools, housing, welfare, and parks, even as it seeks all manner of credit, rebate, subsidy, guarantee, and service from government to "improve the climate for investment."

To cut social spending, capital has employed the old tactics of divide and rule, playing off one segment of the population against the other. Popular prejudice takes greater umbrage at a thousand-dollar welfare cheat than a billion-dollar military swindle. The people close to home always appear to be a greater threat to one's way of life than those who sit in board rooms. Business, and its spokesmen in the press and politics, are always alert to ways to turn this prejudice to advantage.

The drawback to cutting social services is that the gain to capital may prove to be ephemeral. The long-term loss from the disruption of the social order and the waste of human capital may far outweigh the immediate profit. The economics profession in general takes this position, and more perspicacious members of the business community understand the point.

Rohatyn's proposals play on the growing disenchantment with general policies that are confined by practical corporate and political considerations, though he hardly offers a refreshing change. Most planners would agree that wage freezes, tax cuts, and reduced social spending are not enough to ensure economic vigor and social stability. They are ready for planning in earnest.

Such planning will still be for the sake of capital's survival. It will attempt to repair the economy with public works and rebuild mass transit. Government will attempt to develop alternative resources such as solar energy, pay off bionomic debts, and improve the urban environment. But the main thrust of this planning effort will be to establish pervasive taxes, subsidies, and regulations to control resource use, pollution, product design, urban plans, land use, and growth rates for specific industries.

Already there are many examples of this planning effort, even if, in toto, they do not come up to Hubert Humphrey's standards for rationality or coherency. The National Environmental Policy Act requires that before a major project is undertaken, its bionomic costs be accounted for. The act has been used to combat strip mining and introduce auto emission controls. The Nuclear Regulatory Commission has held up licenses for nuclear power plants because of the problem of disposing of radioactive wastes. New York City had been ordered by the federal courts to stop taxi cruising and put tolls on its East River bridges in order to meet clean air standards. General Electric agreed to pay for dumping PCB's into the Hudson River. Throwaway beer cans have been outlawed in several states. The federal government has taken over bankrupt railroads and rescued banks. DDT has been banned. There has been funding for research and subsidies for housing. Wetlands have been ruled off limits to developers. President Carter has proposed stiff penalties for gas-guzzling cars.

Will it work? Will government finally be able to turn the tide by paying for the unprofitable and outlawing the irrational?

Not unless, at the same time, the system can be transformed to account for its limitations. The business community as a whole may agree, eventually, that some strong external direction is necessary for the sake of survival. Yet planning with teeth would put the bite into powerful vested interests. An internal opposition would be set up between the planning sector, representing a type of rationality which capital cannot achieve, and the major corporate interests. Backed by a vigilant public awareness and a sense of national mission, the planning agencies may be strong enough to resist the assimilation process which has befallen regulatory agencies in the past. The planning interests may be able to impose their will, as well as to compromise it, creating strong tensions between the corporate and public domains.

It is difficult, however, to see how these tensions could be workably resolved. Laudable as each project may be, the planning effort as a whole would be at loggerheads with private initiative. The system's basic flaw is its old strength: capital is based on private will, not public purpose. A system that has to be forced to weigh the value of underarm spray deodorants against the possible destruction of the earth's protective ozone layer cannot easily be restructured in the interests of future survival. Remember too that we are not talking of rationalizing a single collective of private capital but a collection of rival and powerful special interests. General Motors or Allied Chemical would not throw in the towel for the sake of preserving capitalism any more than they (or their unions!) would do it to promote the public interest. On the contrary, General Motors used its dominance of the auto and truck industries as a lever to control and destroy the rail and mass transit systems in the United States. Allied Chemical uses its money power to propagandize against government controls over nuclear fuel reprocessing.[25] It is one thing to circumscribe the power of capital; it is quite another to attempt to orient it toward a higher purpose.[26]

The future is closing in on capital. The need for long-run policies and spending to rationalize the economy grows, while it becomes increasingly difficult to accommodate general needs within the old moral and pecuniary framework. The imposition of state control will only heighten the conflict between planning prerogatives and the way in which a profit-oriented market allocates inputs and outputs. Especially under monopoly capitalism, where corporations are political powers in their own right, and where the distinction between regulator and regulatee has become blurred, there can be little hope of establishing an overriding sense of social plan or purpose. Instead, a heavy, bureaucratic dead weight will be set on top of a crumbling market structure.

12

The Death of Capital

The difficulty lies, not in the new ideas, but in escaping from the old ones.

John Maynard Keynes

A short while ago economists were assuring us that they could end poverty and engineer prosperity. Suddenly we are jolted by simultaneous inflation and recession, energy shortages, unemployment, urban decay, and the threat of ecological devastation. This is an especially rude awakening for Americans, who have grown accustomed to new frontiers and rising expectations, and must now adjust to the image of the earth as a small, isolated, fragile planet.

In an age of plutonium reactors and pesticide residues, the word "science" no longer strikes a reassuring chord. This applies doubly to economic science, which stands to be questioned not only in its own right but also for its critical role in shaping all aspects of our social and technical environment. As the good life fades into the smog, there looms a growing concern that the old theories we have come to rely on no longer work, and that no amount of management or manipulation by economists and politicians can bring back stable, prosperous times.

Despite the fact that we live in an atomic age, the existing frame of economic reference is essentially that which was created by Smith, Ricardo, Malthus, and other economists approximately two centuries ago. Their great achievement was to show us how, in a market economy, the quest for individual advantage unintentionally would bring enormous gains in production and trade. According to their theories, unfettered competition was the key to capital's success.

Through greed and fear, competition would spur people into action, guiding the allocation of resources as if by an invisible hand.

The classical demonstration of the invisible hand coincided, in Tawney's words, "with the growth of a political theory which replaced the conception of purpose with that of mechanism." This abdication of theory to mechanism also came at a time when private rights and private interests marched to the tune of industrial expansion and imperial conquest. When there were problems, economists said they were due to too much tampering with the machine.

It would be wrong to oversimplify the classical analysis, since it was intended as a dynamic model, not an attainable, ideal state of society. Nevertheless, the competitive theory was so solid, so reasonable, and so well buttressed by tangible results as to prove a virtually impregnable analytic fortress. True, a number of internal weaknesses and inequities could be pointed out in the model, but even Marx recognized its immediate results. He actually incorporated much of the competitive model in his own analysis, which was based on the growing class tensions created by industrial progress.

But the present malaise affecting capital is somehow different from the business cycles or depressions of the past. Now that the immediate future promises neither harmonious growth nor working class revolt, we have had to reexamine the scientific and institutional preconceptions which underlie the competitive analysis. Once we identified these postulates, we were able to understand the seeming inability of economics to effectively deal with growing problems of resource destruction and the decay of the natural environment, mounting social costs and waste, and the concentration of economic power. In the process, it also became clear that economic theory had overstressed the rationality of the hedonistic motive and had not examined the full implications of perpetual expansion and technological change.

Our faith in self-seeking motives and invisible mechanisms is challenged by urban blight and dreary suburban landscapes. Polluted beaches, decaying transit, ineradicable poverty and rising cancer rates give the lie to our celebrated statistics of rising GNP. Not only is the connection between private choice and social good more tenuous than had been assumed; many economic decisions have little to do with the hedonistic calculus, as big business and government play an increasing role in shaping the economy.

Under conditions of decay, the economic impairment of monopoly may be dwarfed by its political consequences. The presence of large blocks of vested economic power would appear to dash all hopes of rational reconstruction within a market economy. As urban amenities and social order continue to deteriorate, and as the economy comes under increasing resource, bionomic, and structural constraints, government is seen as the only hope to rescue capital and underwrite the consumer economy.

The term "planning" is used to lend scientific credence and liberal respectability to these rescue efforts. But the unreality of these schemes can be seen when we measure the dreams of the planners against the achievements of the Joint National Enterprise to date. Most attempts at government regulation so far, whatever their original intentions, have been co-opted into the service of vested interests. The net result has been a consolidation of bureaucratic control, a further shrinkage of the competitive economy, and a growing predominance of politics over price. Increased muddle and subsidy may be agreeable to the bureaucratic élite and may even enhance the value of proprietary claims, but they also deprive capital of even the pretense of creative function.

The version of planning put forward by the Joint National Enterprise provides only superficial solutions for immediate problems in the attempt to keep up appearances of purposeful growth and economic justice. As politics and economics become locked into a cycle of decline, the market is transformed from a vital decision center into a tool for distributing society's product among competing interests.

The failure of planning to restore the vitality of the classical order signals the death of capital as a creative force. Nor will new solutions be found in the old theories—when power and purpose are divorced, the intellectual bankruptcy of capital becomes as critical as its profit and loss. In our search for new sources of creative energy, we must look beyond capital and the institutional and intellectual frameworks to which it was wed.

Notes

Preface

1. Thorstein Veblen, *Veblen on Marx, Race, Science, and Economics* (New York: Capricorn Books, 1969; originally published in 1919 as *The Place of Science in Modern Civilization and Other Essays*), pp. 341–342.

2. Karl Marx, "Introduction" to his "Grundrisse," printed with *A Contribution to the Critique of Political Economy* (New York: International Publishers, 1970), p. 213.

Part 1 Setting the Stage

Chapter 1 The State of the Art

1. Not every economist is as singleminded as Milton Friedman in defending capitalism against the supposed threat of government regulation and social spending. The man who wrote *Capitalism and Freedom* to argue that only free-market policies can support political democracy now finds himself in the awkward position of being the intellectual mentor of former Chilean students who have become the economic architects for the Pinochet regime. But in this case he denies any connection between economic theory and political repression. Orlando Letelier, "Economic 'Freedom's' Awful Toll," *The Nation,* August 28, 1976.

2. "Book World," *Washington Post,* October 7, 1973.

Chapter 2 The Classical Theory of Capitalism

1. Leo Huberman, *Man's Worldly Goods: The Story of the Wealth of Nations* (New York: Monthly Review Press, 1936, reprinted 1961), p. 105.

2. Ibid., p. 109.

3. Karl Marx, *Capital* (Moscow: Foreign Languages Publishing House, 1961), 1:718.

4. Ibid., pp. 721–724.

5. Adam Smith, *The Wealth of Nations* (New York: Modern Library, 1965), p. 508.

6. Ibid., p. 147.

7. Ibid., p. 355.

8. Adam Smith allowed, of course, that there were certain institutions or works that only benefited society as a whole, whose expense therefore fell upon the sovereign or commonwealth. These were the expenses of defense, of maintaining ministers in foreign countries, of justice, public works, and education. He also allowed for the granting of temporary trade monopolies as well as patents and copyrights.

9. John Stuart Mill, *Principles of Political Economy* (Toronto: University of Toronto Press, 1965), 2:239.

10. Preface (1932) by Berle to Adolf A. Berle and Gardiner C. Means, *The Modern Corporation and Private Property,* rev. ed. (New York: Harcourt Brace & World, 1967), p. xli.

11. Gardiner C. Means, *The Corporate Revolution in America* (New York: Crowell-Collier, 1962), pp. 77–96.

12. Joan Robinson, *The Economics of Imperfect Competition,* 2d. ed. (New York: St. Martin's Press, 1969; originally published in 1933). Edward H. Chamberlin, *The Theory of Monopolistic Competition,* 8th ed. (Cambridge: Harvard University Press, 1962; originally published in 1933).

13. See John M. Blair, *Economic Concentration* (New York: Harcourt Brace Jovanovich, 1972), pp. 228–254.

14. Keynesian political economy was even enacted into law. The Full Employment Act passed by Congress in 1946 made it official policy of the government to do what it reasonably could to ensure jobs for all Americans.

15. John Maynard Keynes, *The General Theory of Employment, Interest, and Money* (New York: Harcourt Brace & World, 1964), p. 378.

16. Paul A. Samuelson, *Economics,* 5th ed. (New York: McGraw-Hill, 1961), p. 38.

17. John Stuart Mill (1806–1873) is often considered to be the last of the great "classical" political economists. The "neoclassical" school which followed dropped the term "political" and adopted a subjective "marginal utility" analysis of competitive equilibrium. The reader can keep this in mind, but for the purposes of the analysis in this book, there is little need to distinguish between the two schools.

Chapter 3 The Marxian Scenarios

1. It is important to emphasize that even though Marx, as a radical philosopher, reversed the Hegelian dialectic in which material progress is but a reflection of man's unfolding spiritual development, and put economic forces at the helm, the dialectic still unfolds through human consciousness and struggle. Not only did Marx examine at length how the historical process unfolds under capitalism, he devoted much of his life to raising the consciousness of working people through writing and organizing: "The dialectic of the movement of social progress [class struggle] . . . moves on the spiritual plane of human desire and passion, not on the (literally) material plane of mechanical and physiological stress, on which the developmental process of brute creation unfolds itself." Veblen, *Veblen on Marx,* p. 415.

2. Marx to Joseph Weydemeyer, March 5, 1852: *Marx, Engels: Selected Correspondence* (Progress Publishers: Moscow, 1975), p. 64.

3. *Economic and Philosophic Manuscripts of 1844,* in Karl Marx and Frederick Engels, *Collected Works* (New York: International Publishers, 1975), 3:267.

4. Karl Marx, *Capital,* 1:270.

5. See Chapter 10.

6. Karl Marx, *Capital* (Moscow: Progress Publishers, 1966), 3:250 (italics in original).

7. Marx, *Capital,* 1:10.

8. Karl Marx, *A Contribution to the Critique of Political Economy* (New York: International Publishers, 1970), p. 21.

9. Marx, *Capital,* 1:762–763.

10. "Competition is often spoken of as if it were necessarily a cause of misery and degradation to the labouring class; as if high wages were not precisely as much a product of competition as low wages." Mill, *Principles of Political Economy,* 2: 216.

11. Karl Marx, *Value, Price and Profit* (New York: International Publishers, 1935), p. 61. Marx argued that in ninety-nine cases out of a hundred, the capitalist will be in a position to raise prices anyway to cover the higher money wages and keep real wages in check.

12. This is not to imply that the classical hedonist analysis is a consistent doctrine. See Chapter 7.

13. Marx, *Capital,* 1:73.

14. Ibid., p. 540.

15. Then too, the apparently democratic forms of politics and culture—less advanced in Marx's day than they are today—that correspond to the capitalist economic form of free exchange (and can be allowed to develop once capitalist production and exchange are established on a firm footing) lend further legitimacy to the prevailing mode of exploitation.

16. Keynes, *The General Theory of Employment, Interest, and Money,* p. 32.

17. Karl Marx, *Theories of Surplus-Value,* pt. 2 (Moscow: Progress Publishers, 1963), p. 500.

18. Ibid., p. 511.

19. Ibid., p. 512.

20. Ibid., p. 520 (italics in original).

21. Marx, *Capital,* 3:484.

22. Marx, *Capital,* 1:614.

23. Among the many examples Marx gives, England's production of cotton cloth was greater in 1868 than in 1861. Yet the number of operatives decreased by 50,000. Marx, *Capital,* 1:434–435.

24. In saying that the most concrete expression of crisis theory is to be found in Chapter 25 of *Capital,* it is by no means implied that Marx had downgraded the intermediate forms, particularly the crisis of overproduction-underconsumption. An understanding of capitalist crisis in all its complexity requires knowledge of how these different forms interact with one another. It is not a question of choosing the best one.

25. Marx, *Capital,* 1:620.

26. Marx, *Value, Price and Profit,* p. 58.

27. Marx believed that the credit system was coming to play an increasingly important role in capitalist expansion and crises, but this does not basically affect our argument here.

28. "Contradiction in the capitalist mode of production: the laborers as buyers of commodities are important for the market. But as sellers of their own commodity —labor-power—capitalist society tends to keep them down to the minimum price." Note by Karl Marx for future amplification in Volume 2 of *Capital* (Moscow: Foreign Languages Publishing House, 1957), p. 316.

29. Ibid., pp. 410–411.

30. It should never be assumed that the existence of a permanent gap between potential and actual output indicates that society is in a chronic state of underconsumption which could be remedied by increased government spending. It simply means that the establishment of the economic equilibrium between supply and demand is dependent on the establishment of a political sway of capital over labor.

31. Keynes, *General Theory of Employment,* pp. 249–250.

32. Of course, we are speaking here of economic stability. Politically, the ax of unemployment might make workers more docile, or the formation of the reserve army could set the stage for rebellion, depending on circumstances.

33. Marx and Engels, "Manifesto of the Communist Party," in *Collected Works,* 6:490.

34. Marx, *Capital,* 1:645.

35. Ibid., p. 621.

36. Marx, *Value, Price and Profit,* p. 61 (italics in original).

Part 2 The Perils of Progress

Chapter 4 The Destruction of Resources

1. U.S. Department of the Interior, *The Fifth Annual Report Council on Environment Quality* (Washington, D.C.: U.S. Government Printing Office, 1974), p. 315.

2. Ibid., p. 342.

3. Ibid., p. 307.

4. Economics is often defined as the study of how society employs scarce resources to achieve its ends. However, this use of the term "scarce" means only that there is an immediate cost of procuring resources, not that there is any planned control over their use.

5. Bernard D. Nossiter, *Soft State* (New York: Harper & Row, 1970), p. xii.

6. Lewis Mumford, *Technics and Civilization* (New York: Harcourt Brace & World, 1934, 1963), p. 81.

7. Robert and Leona Train Rienow, *Moment in the Sun* (New York: Ballantine Books, 1970), p. 162.

8. Ibid., p. 245.

9. Joseph A. Schumpeter, *Capitalism, Socialism and Democracy* (New York: Harper & Row, 1950, 1962), p. 117.

10. Rienow and Rienow, *Moment in the Sun,* p. 240.

11. Ibid., p. 59.

12. S. R. Eyre, "Man the Pest: The Dim Chance of Survival," *New York Review of Books,* November 18, 1971.

13. See Lester R. Brown, *World Population Trends: Signs of Hope, Signs of Stress* (Washington, D.C.: Worldwatch Institute, 1976).

14. Paul R. Ehrlich and John P. Holdren, "Population and Panaceas: A Technological Perspective," in *Global Ecology,* John P. Holdren and Paul R. Ehrlich, eds. (New York: Harcourt Brace Jovanovich, 1971), pp. 14–18.

15. S. R. Eyre, "Man the Pest."

16. Paul R. Ehrlich and John P. Holdren, "Critique," *Science and Public Affairs,* May 1972.

17. Eyre, "Man the Pest."

18. *New York Times,* September 1, 1974.

19. Ibid.

20. Eyre, "Man the Pest."

21. *New York Times,* September 1, 1974.

22. John H. Ryther, "Photosynthesis and Fish Production in the Sea," in Ehrlich and Holdren, *Global Ecology,* p. 36.

23. Eyre, "Man the Pest." p. 21.

24. Ryther, "Photosynthesis," p. 38.

25. Pierre Jalée, *The Third World in World Economy* (New York: Monthly Review Press, 1969), pp. 18–19.

26. "Serious World Food Gap Is Seen over the Long Term by Experts," *New York Times,* December 5, 1976.

27. *Council on Environmental Quality,* p. 312.

28. T. S. Lovering, "Non-Fuel Mineral Resources in the Next Century," in *Global Ecology,* p. 44.

29. Ibid., p. 45.

30. Schumpeter, *Capitalism, Socialism and Democracy,* pp. 115–116.

31. John Kenneth Galbraith, *The New Industrial State* (Boston: Houghton Mifflin, 1967), p. 76.

32. Paul A. Baran and Paul M. Sweezy, *Monopoly Capital* (New York: Monthly Review Press, 1966), p. 48.

33. *New York Times,* February 8, 1976.

Chapter 5 Ecological Suicide

1. "Bionomics" is an old word for "ecology" in the *Oxford English Dictionary*. It would seem appropriate to leave ecology to the ecologists and use the word "bionomics" to specifically apply to the immediate issues which are the joint concern of political economy and ecology.

2. The four laws of ecology are taken from Barry Commoner's book *The Closing Circle* (New York: Alfred A. Knopf, 1971).

3. Ibid., p. 40.

4. Barry Commoner, *Alliance for Survival* (New York: United Electrical, Radio and Machine Workers of America, 1972), p. 13.

5. Ibid., p. 15.

6. According to Joan Robinson, the "stationary state" analysis of Pigou and other neoclassical economists does not permit the introduction of *permanent* losses. *Economic Heresies* (New York: Basic Books, 1971), p. 55.

7. E. J. Mishen, "The Postwar Literature on Externalities: An Interpretative Essay," *Journal of Economic Literature,* March 1971, p. 1.

8. Ibid., p. 26.

9. D. H. Meadows and D. L. Meadows, *The Limits to Growth* (New York: New American Library, 1972), pp. 81–84.

10. Commoner, *Closing Circle,* pp. 144–146.

11. Jack Anderson and Les Whitten, "Crying Over Spilled Oil," New York *Daily News,* January 12, 1977.

12. Commoner, *Closing Circle,* p. 273.

13. Ibid., p. 285.

14. Marx and Engels, "Manifesto of the Communist Party," in *Collected Works* 6:489.

15. Marx, *Capital,* 1:506.

Chapter 6 More Is Less

1. Veblen, *Veblen on Marx,* pp. 145–146.

2. Joan Robinson, *Economic Philosophy* (New York: Anchor Books, 1962), p. 48.

3. Blair, *Economic Concentration,* p. 552.

4. *New York Times,* April 4, 1974.

5. R. H. Tawney, quoting E. F. M. Durbin in *Equality,* 4th ed. rev. (New York: Capricorn Books, 1952, 1961), p. 135.

6. Ibid., p. 134.

7. David Dempsey, "Noise," *New York Times Magazine,* November 23, 1975.

Chapter 7 The Pleasure Principle

1. R. H. Tawney, *The Acquisitive Society* (New York: Harcourt Brace & World, 1920; reprinted 1967), p. 9.

2. Mill, *Principles of Political Economy,* 2:239.

3. Veblen, *Veblen on Marx,* pp. 235–238.

4. Robert J. Lampman, *The Share of Top Wealth-Holders in National Wealth, 1922–1956,* Study by the National Bureau of Economic Research (Princeton, N.J.: Princeton University Press, 1962), pp. 202–209.

5. Thurow, *Generating Inequality,* p. 15.

6. Projector, "Financial Characteristics."

7. Lampman, *Top Wealth-Holders,* pp. 24, 209.

8. Keynes, *General Theory of Employment,* pp. 150–162.

9. Karl Marx, "Introduction" to his "Grundrisse," p. 191.

10. Thorstein Veblen, *The Theory of the Leisure Class* (New York: New American Library, 1953), p. 36.

11. Galbraith, *The New Industrial State,* pp. 179–197.

12. Wesley C. Mitchell, "Lectures on Types of Economic Theory," delivered at the Winter Session, Columbia University, 1934, John M. Myer, ed., stenographic transcription, 1:132–134.

13. Veblen, *Veblen on Marx,* pp. 182–183.

14. Veblen, *Leisure Class,* p. 154.

15. Mumford, *Technics and Civilization,* p. 173.

16. Tawney, *Acquisitive Society,* p. 141.

17. Smith, *The Wealth of Nations,* p. 135.

18. Smith, never an apologist for the bourgeoisie, already recognized that masters generally have the upper hand in wage disputes. Ibid., pp. 66–67.

19. Tawney, *Acquisitive Society,* p. 16.

20. Smith, *Wealth of Nations,* p. 83.

21. Factories may have originally been established more out of the need to establish supervision and discipline than to advance the division of labor and introduce machine processes (as in Smith's pin factory).

22. Tawney, *Acquisitive Society,* p. 143.

23. For an examination of the contemporary labor process, see Harry Braverman, *Labor and Monopoly Capital* (New York: Monthly Review Press, 1974).

24. "The industrial worker has served as a guinea pig for environmental problems. Industrial chemicals that pollute the environment are much more concentrated in

the plant, so that the worst and earliest effects will be experienced by the workers in the plant." Commoner, *Alliance for Survival,* p. 22.

25. Joel Seligman, "Our Corporate Commissars," *The Nation,* June 12, 1976.

26. Joseph R. Daughen and Peter Binzen, *The Wreck of the Penn Central* (New York: New American Library), pp. 122–149.

27. Mumford, *Technics and Civilization,* pp. 153–154.

Chapter 8 The Corporate Domain

1. Veblen, *Veblen on Marx,* p. 173.

2. Robinson, *Economic Philosophy,* p. 147. We assume there is no technical reason why firms must remain small.

3. Thorstein Veblen, *The Theory of Business Enterprise* (New York: The New American Library, 1968), p. 29.

4. New York *Times,* April 26, 1974.

5. "One must quite naturally hesitate about speaking of a 'public interest' or a 'public utility' which is carried on the books of a private corporation as a capitalised source of income." Thorstein Veblen, *Absentee Ownership* (Boston: Beacon Press, 1923, 1967), p. 172.

6. *Concentration Ratios in Manufacturing,* U.S. Department of Commerce, Bureau of the Census (Washington, D.C.: U.S. Government Printing Office, 1975).

7. The method of classification is that used by John M. Blair in analyzing 1963 concentration data, *Economic Concentration,* p. 13.

8. "Fortune 500," *Fortune,* May, 1975.

9. *Fortune,* July, 1973.

10. *Washington Post,* October 3, 1971.

11. Senate Committee on Government Operations, *Disclosure of Corporate Ownership* (Washington, D.C.: U.S. Government Printing Office, 1974), pp. 135–136.

12. Ibid., p. 137.

13. Ibid., pp. 55–57.

14. Blair, *Economic Concentration,* pp. 75–81.

15. *Disclosure of Corporate Ownership,* p. 385.

16. Robert Sherrill, "Breaking Up Big Oil," *New York Times Magazine,* October 3, 1976.

17. Alfred W. Stonier and Douglas C. Hague, *A Textbook of Economic Theory* (New York: John Wiley & Sons, 1964), p. 170.

18. Ibid., pp. 171–172.

19. A number of Means's earlier essays, including those on administered pricing, are reproduced in *The Corporate Revolution in America.*

20. Ibid., p. 78.

21. Blair, *Economic Concentration,* pp. 228–254.

22. Chamberlin, *The Theory of Monopolistic Competition,* pp. 162–169.

23. Joan Robinson, *The Economics of Imperfect Competition* (New York: St Martin's Press, 1969), pp. 217–320.

24. Gardiner C. Means testified before Senator Estes Kefauver's Senate Antitrust and Monopoly Subcommittee on the problem of "Administrative Inflation" back in 1957—seventeen years prior to the White House Conference on the newly discovered problem of "stagflation." See *Corporate Revolution,* pp. 101–129.

25. Veblen, *The Theory of Business Enterprise,* pp. 18–36.

26. The old steam-powered industrial technology, though more flexible than the water-powered one which preceded it, drew manufacturing processes in around the source. Electrical power, which can be dispersed and transmitted over great distances, permits industrial diffusion. In transport, the replacement of railroads by trucks has had an added decentralizing effect by dispersing material flows into smaller regional and local patterns. In materials, steel is being replaced by fiberglass-reinforced plastics and prestressed concrete, which can be fabricated cheaply by small plants. Machines, which used to be highly specialized and suited only to high-volume, standardized production, are being replaced by flexible, multipurpose ones that can be adapted to a variety of outputs. Even computers are no longer a luxury that only big corporations can afford. The latest advances in miniaturization, software, and time sharing are putting electronic accounting and information handling capabilities within the reach of all but the smallest firms. (John M. Blair, "The New Industrial Revolution," *The Nation,* June 12, 1972.)

27. Bradford C. Snell, *American Ground Transport, A Proposal for Restructuring the Automobile, Truck, Bus, and Rail Industries,* Senate Subcommittee on Antitrust and Monopoly (Washington, D.C.: U.S. Government Printing Office, 1974), pp. A–50–51. General Motors has vigorously denied having orchestrated the demise of the trolley car systems and has argued that these failed on their own accord. "The Truth About 'American Ground Transport'—A Reply by General Motors," pp. A–107–127.

28. Ibid., p. A–30.

29. Ibid., p. A–31.

30. Jack Anderson, New York *Post,* January 15, 1974.

31. *New York Times,* February 14, 1974.

32. Ibid., April 7, 1974.

Chapter 9 The Last Great Merger

1. Jack Anderson, New York *Post,* January 15, 1974.

2. *New York Times,* January 7, 1974.

3. The excuse for sacrificing Alaska to the oil giants was to make America "energy independent." It seemed a bit suspicious that the oil companies insisted on running the pipeline from Prudhoe Bay to the sea at Valdez, Alaska, rather than direct to the oil-short Midwest, even though California had little need for high-sulphur crude.

Oil ran thicker than reason, however, and the Congress acquiesced, but not before writing an export prohibition into law.

Now that work is under way, the oil companies are letting it be known that there is a looming glut of crude on the West Coast; that we had better ship the stuff to Japan, before we drown in it (*New York Times,* November 28, 1976). The political machine will take a lot of greasing before it cranks this one out!

4. *New York Times,* February 26, 1974.

5. Jack Anderson, "Nixon's Oil Mistakes," *New York Post,* October 8, 1974.

6. *New York Times,* February 21, 1974.

7. *New York Times,* February 28, 1974.

8. The oil giants claimed illegal tax deductions on millions of dollars of "nonpolitical" ads criticizing the Clean Air Act, calling for the deregulation of natural gas, attacking auto emission standards or opposing the proposed excess profit tax. New York *Post,* May 7, 1974.

9. James Nathan Miller, "They're Giving Us Gas, All Right," *New Republic,* February 12, 1977.

10. Clayton Fritchey, "To Deregulate—Or Not?" Washington *Post,* February 12, 1977.

11. "Ma Bell's Consumer Reform Bill," *Consumer Reports,* January, 1977.

12. Ibid.

13. Mill, *Principles of Political Economy,* 5:970.

14. Ibid., 5:803.

15. Robinson, *Economic Philosophy,* pp. 97–100.

16. "Industry Effects of Government Expenditures: An Input-Output Analysis," *Survey of Current Business,* May, 1975.

17. Our chart shows each industry in terms of employment. Government expenditures were $636 billion in 1976, an amount equal to 38 percent of the Gross National Product. *Survey of Current Business,* January, 1977.

18. Thorstein Veblen, *Absentee Ownership* (Boston: Beacon Press, 1923, 1967), p. 22.

19. Charles A. Beard, *An Economic Interpretation of the Constitution of the United States* (New York: Macmillan, 1913, 1956).

Part 3 The Fading Ideal

Chapter 10 Growth . . . and Decay

1. Smith, *Wealth of Nations,* pp. 94–95.

2. David Ricardo, *Principles of Political Economy and Taxation* (Baltimore: Penguin Books, 1971), p. 291.

3. Mill, *Principles of Political Economy,* book 4.

4. Keynes, *General Theory,* p. 374.

5. Marx, *Capital,* 3:211–266.

6. Schumpeter, *Capitalism, Socialism and Democracy,* p. 131.

7. Ibid., p. 134.

8. Veblen, *Absentee Ownership,* p. 102.

9. Ibid., p. 421–422.

10. John M. Blair, *The Control of Oil* (New York: Pantheon Books, 1976), p. 329.

11. Michael T. Klare, "The Boom in Private Police," *The Nation,* November 15, 1975.

12. The manufacture of transportation equipment, for example, had to be divided between intermediate and personal use, even though it is impossible to precisely divide the use of cars and trucks between business and pleasure.

13. Joan Robinson, "The Age of Growth," *Challenge,* May–June, 1976, p. 9.

14. Mill, *Principles of Political Economy,* 4:756.

Chapter 11 The Inevitability of Planning

1. Paul M. Sweezy, *The Theory of Capitalist Development* (New York: Monthly Review Press, c. 1942, 1956), pp. 53–54. A recent statement by Sweezy: "I used to think that important principles were involved in the market vs. plan question, but I no longer do." *Papers and Proceedings,* Eighty-ninth Annual Meeting of the American Economic Association, *The American Economic Review,* February, 1977, p. 67.

2. E. G. Liberman, *Economic Methods and the Effectiveness of Production* (Garden City, New York: Anchor Books, 1973), p. 67.

3. See Ota Šik, *Plan and Market under Socialism* (White Plains, N.Y.: International Arts and Sciences Press, 1967).

4. "National Economic Planning: Pro and Con," *New York Times,* December 21, 1975.

5. Schumpeter, *Capitalism, Socialism and Democracy,* p. 137.

6. Walton Hamilton, *The Politics of Industry* (New York: Vintage Books, 1957), p. 52.

7. Louis M. Kohlmeier, "When Regulators Enlist with the Regulated," *New York Times,* August 1, 1976.

8. *New York Times,* November 18, 1976.

9. *Congressional Record,* H2660-3, April 4, 1974.

10. *New York Times,* October 3, 1976.

11. Representative Henry S. Reuss, "A Private Club for Public Policy," *The Nation,* October 16, 1976.

12. Blair, *Control of Oil,* p. 399.

13. Corporate planning is so intertwined with government planning that it is almost double-counting to mention it. Every business on the *Fortune* lists has its own staff of planners, forecasters, and market researchers. In addition, there are a host of organizations, firms, and consultants who specialize in planning services for businesses. Major corporations do not merely predict and adapt to the future; they administer prices and carry out well-coordinated campaigns using both the market and political weapons at their disposal.

14. "Javits/Humphrey Propose Legislation for Long-Term Economic Planning," Press release from the office of Senator Jacob K. Javits, May 12, 1975.

15. Ibid.

16. Letter on French Planning to *Challenge,* March–April 1976, p. 67.

17. In New York we have the sublime spectacle of closed hospitals and firehouses, halted school and subway construction, at the very time when government is channeling billions of dollars into such Rockefeller-sponsored "pyramid building" as the World Trade Center, the Albany Mall, the Roosevelt Island complex, Battery Park City, and the Westway, a six-lane covered highway down the West Side of Manhattan.

18. "A New R.F.C. Is Proposed for Business," *New York Times,* December 1, 1974.

19. Ibid.

20. "[O]nly hours after the Government granted $730 million in shipbuilding loan guarantees to General Dynamics [presumably the type of "planning" Rohatyn is talking about], Lazard appeared as the lead underwriter for $250 million in securities floated on behalf of General Dynamics to finance its shipbuilding program." *New York Times,* January 30, 1977.

21. British Prime Minister James Callaghan carried this argument to the international level. He warned foreign creditors not to press Britain too hard with austerity demands as a condition for new loans, the implication being that if Britain could not pay back investors, the United States, West Germany, or the International Monetary Fund would be forced to back up Britain's sterling liabilities in order to avoid international financial chaos. *New York Times,* October 27, 1976.

22. An interesting, if somewhat more modest, example of how the public underwrites the private sector has been given by the recent efforts of several utility companies to bill their customers, in advance, for the funds to build power plants or tap new supplies of natural gas. The customers then will bear the double indignity of supplying capital to the utilities and then being billed for the dividends!

23. "Corporate Taxes Wither Away," *Dollars and Sense,* April 1976, pp. 2–3.

24. Joseph A. Pechman and Benjamin A. Okner, *Who Bears the Tax Burden?* (Washington, D.C.: Brookings Institution, 1974), pp. 4–10.

25. See, for example, its ad in the *New York Review of Books,* March 17, 1977, p. 13.

26. "In the face of this situation—social problems pressing for attention, corporations challenged to exercise social responsibility but having little capacity to do anything singly and captained by individuals who still believe deeply in the values

of which their organizations are the chief carriers—what response can one expect? What else but a limited response? Modest concessions, within the realm of the corporation's limited discretion. Incremental changes in corporate policies and conduct, as long as these do not entail differential costs that jeopardize competitive performance. A public relations program designed to reassure uneasy segments of the public that their concerns are not being ignored." Neil W. Chamberlain, *The Limits of Corporate Responsibility* (New York: Basic Books, 1973), p. 202.

INDEX

About the Author

Stephen E. Harris has been educated at Goddard College, Howard University, and the London School of Economics. He is an Associate Staff Analyst for the City of New York and a doctoral candidate in political economy at the New School for Social Research.